THE ART OF EGYPT THROUGH THE AGES

Printed and Engraved in Great Britain by
H. Reiach Ltd., 43 Belvedere Road, S.E.1
Photogravure plates by Art Photogravure
Company, Ltd., Park Royal Road, N.W.10

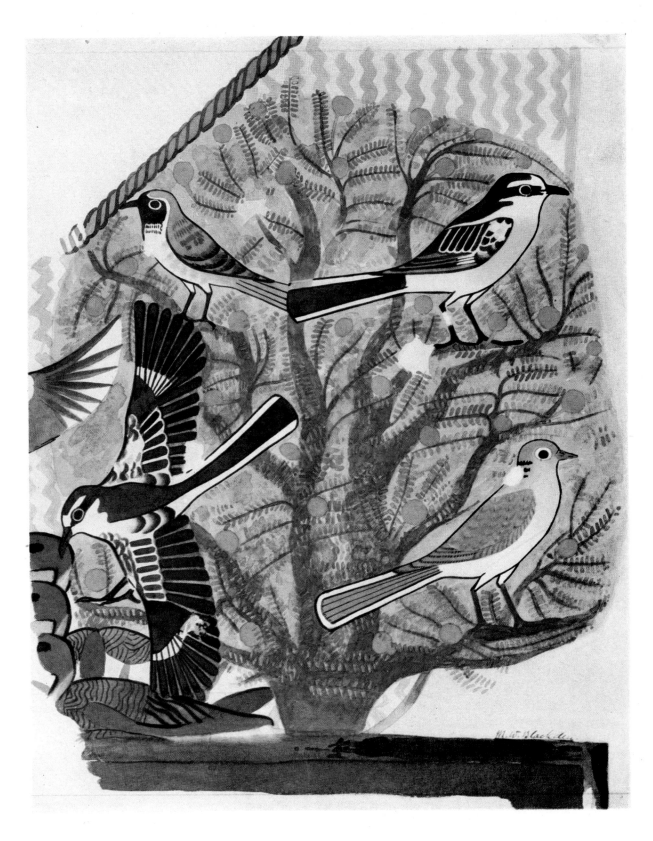

BIRDS PERCHED ON THE BRANCHES OF AN ACACIA TREE
FROM A PAINTING IN THE TOMB-CHAPEL OF KHNEMḤOTPE
AT BENI ḤASAN
Reproduced from a water-colour drawing by M. W. Blackden.
By courtesy of the Egypt Exploration Society.

THE ART OF EGYPT

THROUGH THE AGES

Edited by

SIR E. DENISON ROSS, C.I.E., Ph.D., etc.

Director of the School of Oriental Studies

1931

THE STUDIO LTD.

44 LEICESTER SQUARE, LONDON, W.C.2

TO

HIS MAJESTY

KING FUAD

WHO HAS DONE SO MUCH

TO FOSTER ART AND LETTERS

IN MODERN EGYPT

THIS TRIBUTE

TO THE ARTISTIC GENIUS

OF THAT GREAT COUNTRY

IS RESPECTFULLY

DEDICATED

ACKNOWLEDGEMENTS

The Editor and Publishers desire to express their thanks to His Excellency Dr. Hafez Afifi Pasha, the Egyptian Minister in London, to the Members of the Egyptian Legation and to those Officials of Museums and Public Galleries and Private Collectors who have kindly assisted in the preparation of this book.

In particular, they wish to express their thanks to M. Georges Cattaui, whose enthusiasm and counsel have been a constant help ; to the Baroness d'Erlanger ; to M. Lacau, Directeur-Général du Service des Antiquités at Cairo, and to Mr. Cecil Firth ; to M. Gaston Wiet, Director of the Arab Museum at Cairo ; Professor Sir Flinders Petrie and Miss Margaret Murray, of University College, London ; to Dr. Robert Mond, President, and Miss Jonas, Secretary, of the Egypt Exploration Society, Dr. E. T. Leeds, Keeper of the Ashmolean Museum, Dr. Alan Gardiner and Professor Reisner, Director of the Harvard-Boston Egyptian Expedition.

It is with the most profound regret that they have to record the death of Sir Thomas Arnold and Dr. H. R. Hall ; they wish to thank very warmly Mrs. R. H. Devonshire, who kindly consented to edit and complete the notes which Sir Thomas Arnold left for his unfinished article on the Arts and Crafts of Muslim Egypt, and Mr. S. R. K. Glanville of the British Museum, by whom the proofs of Dr. Hall's chapter on the Old Kingdom have been corrected and the illustrations to it finally selected and arranged.

Special thanks for their advice and assistance and for their courtesy in allowing their collections to be drawn upon for material, are also due to H.H. Prince Youssef Kamal, Mr. A. Chester Beatty, M. Jacques Cartier, Mr. E. Disney, M. l'Abbé Drioton, Mr. Ralph Harari, Mr. Rhuvon Guest, M. Gulbenkian, Captain Ingram, M. Dikran Kelekian, Mr. Bernard Rackham, Mr. Herbert Read and Mr. A. J. B. Wace.

CONTENTS

COLOUR PLATES

INTRODUCTION

EGYPT is the cradle of the arts, and were it not for the survival of so many of her early monuments the opening chapters of the history of Art would be largely based on conjecture. With every addition to our knowledge of her achievements, the debt to Egypt of all later arts becomes more apparent. Only recently, for example, have researches at Sakkara definitely proved that the fluted column was first evolved by the Egyptian architects. No less important and far-reaching was the influence of Egypt on human thought : her archives moreover are the oldest treasure-house of the history of mankind.

When ancient Egypt first began to occupy the attention of the West, the linguist and the historian were the interpreters of her civilization, and the æsthetic value of her monuments was hardly recognized. Hieroglyphs were deciphered and read, but our classical and modern prejudices hindered us from appreciating an art so essentially unfamiliar. It took the artistic world long to rid itself of the obsession of Hellenic formulæ, and to approach the masterpieces of the Pharaohs with an open and impartial mind. Nowadays, we have learnt to accept Egyptian art forms without self-consciousness or shyness, and if our reaction to these is in any way restrained, it is due to the stereotyped formality of the Egyptians, which in European art belongs only to its early phases. The wonder is that in spite of such rigid stylization the Egyptian artists were able throughout so many centuries to continue to produce original masterpieces. It must be realized that art in Egypt was so inextricably bound up with religion that when the old religion was supplanted by a new one the old art likewise disappeared, and it is curious to speculate how Pharaonic art might have developed had it survived the old religion. Perhaps the answer is ready to hand, and is to be found in classical art. At any rate, the old art disappears entirely from the valley of the Nile with the arrival of the Arabs and the spread of Islam.

It must not, however, be forgotten that side by side with the religious buildings, sculptures and paintings, there flourished in Egypt the domestic arts and that these, being secular, survived the eclipse of the Egyptian religion.

It is here that we may trace a continuity of style and technique persisting through the Greco-Roman, the Coptic and the Islamic periods. The same procedure is to be observed in Persia, where the conversion of the country to Islam brought about a complete change in her public buildings, the mosque superseding the temple, while the textiles, pottery, and metalwork carried on the pre-Islamic tradition. It is, however, strange that the builders of Coptic churches and of Muslim mosques in Egypt should have remained utterly uninfluenced by the glorious architecture of the ancient Egyptians with which they were of course perfectly familiar.

The earliest connected history of Egypt known to us was written in the third century B.C. by an Egyptian priest named Manetho in the service of Ptolemy Philadelphus. This work, written in Greek, contained a complete history of the Pharaohs from the time when Upper and Lower Egypt were first united in a single kingdom. Unfortunately nothing of this work has survived except the dynastic tables. Until the interpretation of Egyptian hieroglyphs made original researches possible, our knowledge of Egyptian history was based on these tables and on the Greek historians from Herodotus onwards. Manetho records upwards of twenty dynasties, naming them after the various nomes or districts from which these dynastic families came. Later scholars found it convenient to give numbers rather than names to these dynasties ; and these they arranged in three main groups corresponding with the three main periods of Egyptian greatness : namely, the Old Kingdom (Manetho's First to Sixth Dynasties), the Middle Kingdom (Manetho's Eleventh and Twelfth), and the New Kingdom (Manetho's Eighteenth and Nineteenth). The long period of foreign Hyksos domination includes the Thirteenth to Seventeenth Dynasties. Much doubt still prevails regarding the probable dates to be assigned to the early dynasties. Suffice it to say that Menes, the first king mentioned by Manetho, probably lived in the middle of the fourth Millenium B.C., and that the Twelfth Dynasty, under which the sceptres of Upper and Lower Egypt were united, arose about 2000 B.C. When Egyptologists speak of the Predynastic times they mean those periods represented by archæological remains belonging to an age anterior to the first dynasty known to Manetho.

Our knowledge of Predynastic Egypt is constantly being enlarged, as for example by the recent finds at Badari, which suddenly carried us back to a highly-developed civilization older than any we had hitherto known.

I may be permitted in this place to quote from a letter written recently to "The Times" by the great pioneer, Sir Flinders Petrie, the founder of Egyptian archæology in England, who has devoted fifty years of untiring zeal and energy to the work of exploration.

" In 1880, when I began work in Egypt, there was no link with the west before the Greek traditions, there was nothing known in Egypt itself older than the Great Pyramid, and we knew no objects of the most usual material civilization. Our understanding of Palestine and Babylonia was in an even worse plight.

" Stage by stage our mist of ignorance has been rolled back, and dozens of students have taken part with me in this enterprise. Contact of Egypt with the west has been traced through all the ages of prehistoric Greece. In Egypt itself the whole course of recorded history is now before us, and the beautiful things of the early monarchy are much better known than those of the Saxons in England. Before all written record, four successive civilizations are known in detail, and a fifth has come to view."

In the light of recent discoveries of other ancient civilizations it must be admitted that the art of Egypt was purely local in origin, although here and there we find a breaking away from accepted conventions, even in comparatively early times, as for example in the sculptor of the statue of Mesekhti, and in the paintings of the vanished tombs of Beni Hasan.

The political disorganization which characterized the end of the Old Empire led to a period of marking-time in matters of art. The Middle Empire witnessed the resuscitation of the old workshops, but the artists of this period, instead of bringing about a renaissance, sank back into a formalism which reminds one of the stylization of the Buddha figures of Gandhara, giving the impression of taking everything from art and nothing from nature.

The end of the Twelfth Dynasty seems to have witnessed a revival of the artistic standards of the Old Kingdom. The sculptors of the Twelfth Dynasty had a style of their own, which might be called realistic in its attempt to portray the emotions as well as the features. Special attention must be called to the two portraits of Amenemḥēt III, which certainly stand out as real triumphs of the Egyptian genius. The Old Kingdom also gave us that wonderful statue in wood called the Sheikh El-Beled.

During the period of the domination of the Hyksos kings, a considerable break occurred in Egyptian art, though it would seem that these alien rulers did not actually prevent the Egyptian artists from prosecuting their calling. With the expulsion of the Hyksos began a totally new era in art, and the monarchs of the Eighteenth and Nineteenth Dynasties were more devoted to the erection of great monuments than those of any other period : and in this they were no doubt greatly aided by the presence of so many captives in the land.

When in 525 B.C. Cambyses conquered Egypt, this country had already existed for about 6,000 years, and during the two hundred years of their rule, the Persians seem to have exercised no influence at all over Egypt. They were, however, quick to borrow from the Egyptians, as is very evident from the ruins of their palaces in Persepolis and elsewhere. When Alexander the Great conquered Egypt towards the end of the fourth century B.C., Greek art was at the height of its excellence, and Alexandria became the centre of interest. Under the Ptolemies (Lagids) architecture of a somewhat theatrical type flourished, as witness the temples of Dendereh, Edfu, Phylæ, etc., but sculpture lost nearly all value. It is interesting to note that the " Greco-Roman " paintings which begin to appear in the second century A.D. are a genuine product of Egypt. This style of painting has never been found elsewhere, and the type is mainly Levantine.

The period between the battle of Actium, when Egypt became part of the Roman Empire, 31 B.C., and the Arab Invasion in the seventh century A.D. is but little known, and it is curious to watch the gradual disappearance of the Pharaonic civilization. Hieroglyphs have been found as late as the third century A.D. and the worship of Isis in Phylæ was only suppressed by Justinian in the sixth century A.D.

Among the arts which seem to have persisted in Egypt throughout the ages are those of weaving and embroidery, for though new designs from all over the East—even from distant China—were always welcomed, a high level of skill was always maintained, and so distinctive were their local adaptations that it is often difficult to discriminate between Coptic and Early Muslim work. It is worthy of note that if Egypt remained immune from Mongol invasion the conquest of the rest of Islamic Asia by the Mongols led to another kind of invasion of Egypt by artists and artisans of Mesopotamia and Persia, who introduced much that was new into Egypt, as for example, the metal-work of Mosul.

It was Ibn Tūlūn in the ninth century who revived the native glory of Egypt ; and it was under the Fatimids (tenth-eleventh century) that Cairo became the intellectual metropolis of orthodox Islam which, thanks to the great University of Al-Azhar, it has remained ever since.

E. DENISON ROSS

THE PREDYNASTIC AND
EARLY DYNASTIC PERIOD

FORTY years ago the history of Egypt began with the Fourth Dynasty. It was indeed obvious that behind the dynasty which built the greatest of the pyramids and produced some of the most perfect portrait-statues the world has ever seen there must lie a long period of civilisation, and a long apprenticeship to the arts of sculpture and architecture ; yet of this period little was known save the names of a few of its kings Excavation has altered all this. Not only has it filled in the main lines of the history of the first three dynasties and furnished us with examples of their art, but it has revealed to us an even earlier period, commonly known as the Predynastic, behind which lie the Badarian and Tasian epochs, which show us still more primitive stages in the development of Egyptian art. It is the purpose of this chapter to trace these early beginnings and to show how they led up to the fully formed art of the Old Kingdom.

It is neither possible nor necessary to put any very precise dating upon the objects which are here to be described. Suffice it to say that in the opinion of most Egyptologists the beginning of the Dynastic Period is to be placed somewhere not very long before 3000 B.C. The length of the periods which precede it, the Predynastic, the Badarian and the Tasian, is a matter of the purest conjecture ; some would assign to them four or five centuries, others as much as two thousand years. We do not know, and it is possible that we never shall know.

It is an axiom of a certain school of anthropological thought that art for art's sake is a conception wholly foreign to the primitive mind. This may be literally true ; it is hard to believe that the men of the Upper Palæolithic period in North Spain covered the walls of pitch-dark caverns with paintings of animals merely from a sense of decoration. Even in Egypt of the historical periods, the portrait statues which we so much admire were made not as works of art but to be buried in the tomb, where they might serve to take the place of the body, should this perish. Moreover, the further we go back into Predynastic times the rarer become objects which have been made from a purely artistic sense, and the more rarely do common objects bear a decoration which is purely æsthetic, and has no useful or magical motive. This is an important principle, which must be constantly kept in mind if the nature of the earliest art of Egypt is to be properly understood.

This being so, it is clear that any attempt to divide the art of early Egypt into useful and decorative would be a mistake. A much more suitable division, which we shall adopt here, is the division into representative and non-representative. Representative art is that which attempts to reproduce or imitate something which already exists in nature or manufacture. Thus modelling and sculpture are representative arts, for they reproduce the figures of men, animals and inanimate objects. So, too, are painting and incising, for the craftsman must paint or incise something, otherwise he is not an artist. On the other hand, the arts of the architect, the potter, the stone-vase maker and the jeweller are non-representative; all these create things which are not necessarily copies of anything which exists. When, however, the artist proceeds to add statues or reliefs to a building, or paints scenes on a vase, or gives to his bracelet the form of a bird or animal, he passes over into the realm of representative art. Thus the two types of art, representative and non-representative, may easily, and often do, cross each other's boundaries. Nevertheless, this does not take away from the usefulness of the division for practical purposes, and we shall have no hesitation in adopting it in the present chapter.

REPRESENTATIVE ART. In view of the large and admirable part which sculpture played in the history of Egyptian art, we may not unreasonably put it first in our treatment of the representative arts. The evidence of the Badarian and predynastic tombs makes it quite clear that it had its rise in the modelling of human and animal figures in Nile mud. These early models were probably not made as toys for children, much as their appearance might suggest this ; they are found in tombs, and were doubtless placed there in order to furnish the dead man, through those magic means with which we are so familiar in later Egypt, with the numbers of the objects figured which he might require in his second life.

Among the crudest and yet most striking of these figures are the steatopygous female figurines of clay found at Naqadah and other sites (P. 82). The purpose of these and the reason of their peculiar configuration are still unknown, but they certainly reveal a very primitive stage in the representation of the human figure. To an almost equally early stage belong some of the figures of animals, chiefly oxen, found at El-Amrah (P. 83). As works of art these figures are almost without merit. All the artist has done is to indicate, usually by exaggeration, the salient feature of the anatomy of his subject.

Along with these appear figures of another type, distinguished by their long stiff lines. These early figures are generally cut in ivory, and their form may be partly due to the grain of the material. In them, however, there is some attempt to reproduce the human features (P. 84, fig. 1). A more developed form of this type of art is seen in the famous basalt figure now in the Ashmolean Museum (P. 84, fig. 2). Here, despite the stiff and awkward lines, there is real characterisation in the features ; the mastery over the material is almost complete, and the technical skill very great. The same cleverness in portraying racial characteristics in the features which served the Egyptian artist so well in later times is seen in the little lapis lazuli figurine from Hieraconpolis (P. 84, fig. 3), though this is in other respects a less finished work than the basalt figure.

The promise held out by these two figures is seen fulfilled in the wonderful collection of ivory figurines (P. 85, figs. 1, 3, and fig. 1 below) found in the votive deposit at Hieraconpolis. The date of these is not fixed by the circumstances of their finding, but we need have no hesitation in assigning them to the beginnings of the Dynastic Period. The sad condition in which they were extricated from the soil makes it in some cases difficult to appreciate their artistic value ; some, however, are well enough preserved to show that we are in the presence of a very finished school of carving, with complete mastery over its material. A wonderful statuette of a king wearing the crown of Upper Egypt, found at Abydos, belongs to the same school, and is perhaps the most perfect of its products (P. 87, fig. 2).

Curiously enough, this fine work has left us no counterpart in the larger forms of sculpture. The great statues of the god Min from Coptos (P. 86, fig. 2) and the similar figure from Hieraconpolis attach themselves by the rigidity and crudeness of their forms rather to the stiff ivory figurines of the type shown in P. 84, fig. 1, than to these finer works. A figure of an ape inscribed with the name of Narmer, in the Berlin Museum, is perhaps a fair specimen of the sculptor's skill at the beginning of the First Dynasty, but there must be several transition stages between this and the remarkably finished statues of Khasekhem of the Second Dynasty, stages which may any day be revealed to us by excavation (P. 86, fig. 1).

Side by side with this development in sculpture in the round went a similar improvement in the cutting of reliefs. These are best known to us from three series of objects, ivory handles for flint knives, slate palettes and ceremonial mace-heads. The knife-handles as a whole are probably the earliest of the three, for, while the palettes and mace-heads bring us to the verge of the Dynastic Period, the knife-handles can be dated, by means of the ripple-

Fig. 1. Two of the ivory figurines from the votive deposit at Hieraconpolis. From Quibell and Green "Hieraconpolis."

7

flaked knives to which some of them are still attached, to the Middle Predynastic Period.

The earliest of the knife-handles are doubtless those which show groups of animals in procession (P. 87, fig. 1), possibly connected with the totemistic survivals which seem to be observable in early Egypt. This type of decoration was applied not only to knife-handles but to other objects in ivory, such as combs (P. 87, fig. 3). In many of these the work is very fine and delicate, and although the forms of the animals are not perfect the characterisation is good. But the culmination of this type of work is seen in the ivory knife-handle from Gebel 'Araq, now in the Louvre (P. 88, fig. 1). The fineness of the work and the sureness of the artist's hand make this one of the masterpieces of the early art of the world.

The great slate palettes, probably ceremonial embellishments of the simple palettes used for grinding eye-paint, form a series which enables us to watch the development of the art of sculpture in relief. In the earliest, or at any rate the crudest, that of the huntsmen, the human figure is very roughly treated, though the artist is more at home with animals. In the great animal palette (P. 88, fig. 2) we see early signs of that adroitness in adapting a subject to the space at his disposal which was throughout one of the Egyptian decorative artist's chief merits; and the two giraffes feeding off a palm tree on the London and Oxford palette (P. 87, fig. 4) well illustrate another of his gifts, namely a wonderful feeling for what is known as " line." In technical excellence, however, all these are surpassed by the great Narmer palette (P. 90, fig. 1); here we see clever composition, a keen sense of decorative effect, and delicate rendering of detail; there is even some attempt at modelling the almost flat surfaces and at indicating the muscles. At the same time we must not exaggerate the qualities of this work of art; it has a stiffness, an awkwardness and a lack of life which make it rank far behind the best work of the Old Kingdom.

To the same category belong the decorated limestone mace-heads, two of which bear the names of the Scorpion King and Narmer respectively. In these an even more difficult task has been successfully accomplished, namely the adaptation of a free design to a rapidly curving surface. The photograph of the Scorpion King's mace-head given on P. 89 will show how far the technical skill and decorative sense of the early Egyptian were ahead of his knowledge of perspective and his treatment of movement.

Unfortunately the stages which separate these early reliefs from the admirable work shown in the wooden panels of Hesy and the doorways of King Zoser in the Third Dynasty are mostly lost, and we have little to fill the gap except the beautifully designed and perfectly cut stela of the Serpent King in the First Dynasty, which, while it proves an even further advance in technical ability, does not show any development in power of representing life and movement (P. 91).

Only one piece of predynastic painting of any extent has come down to us. It is on the walls of a tomb at Hieraconpolis. The objects represented include human figures, animals and boats. The drawing is very poor and the colours are crude.

At the same time we have ample opportunities of judging the proficiency of the Egyptian predynastic draughtsman and painter from the application of their arts to the decoration of pottery. Two types of early pottery in particular depended upon painted ornament; in the one the designs were carried out in matt white paint on a polished red background, while in the other, which is as a whole rather later in date, the background is of an unpolished buff colour, and the ornament is in dull red. In both types of ware some of the designs are simple, and to all appearance purely geometric, though here, too, we must remember the dictum of many anthropologists that no primitive design is purely ornamental, but that each has its origin in something natural. Thus the red blotches which decorate some of the buff vases are clearly intended to imitate the markings of the pink breccia from which vases of the same form were often made, and the spirals which are similarly used may well have been suggested by coils of rope. So, too, the cross-line decoration which is particularly common in the white-on-red ware, as also in the black ware with white-filled incision, is almost certainly derived from patterns natural to basket-work. From the artistic point of view, however, the interest of this vase-painting lies chiefly in the more ambitious designs which reproduce natural objects such as birds, animals, fish, and even men. In the earliest white-on-red vases these are exceedingly crude (P. 93, fig. 1), especially when the human figure is concerned. In the better red-on-buff vases, however, there is a considerable advance, though even here there is still much that is very primitive. Men, animals and ships are intermingled almost without scheme (P. 94, fig. 2-3), and the artists' only idea of composition seems often to have been to cover the available space as completely as possible by the insertion of meaningless hooks and zigzags where there was room for nothing larger.

NON-REPRESENTATIVE ART. Those forms of art which aimed at the production of something new rather than at the imitation of something already existing were on the whole of more importance to primitive man than the others. A hut to live in, a tomb to be buried in, clothes to wear, and pots and pans in which to cook his food were all necessities, and yet necessities capable of being elaborated into luxuries. Thus it was that the making of these necessities developed into the various arts.

Of the architecture of primitive Egypt we know but little, for both houses and temples have perished, and only tombs remain. From these, however, we learn that long before the First Dynasty unbaked bricks of Nile mud had come into use. The tomb of King Den of the First Dynasty is the earliest known example of the use of stone in Egyptian architecture, and even here the granite blocks are only used for the floor of the sepulchral pit ; yet we may be certain that a people who could work granite into blocks must already have been using stone for their palaces and their temples, if not for their houses. All these, however, have disappeared, and there is nothing left save a clay model from a tomb at El-'Amrah to tell us what the early house looked like. From this, and from various survivals in the stone buildings of later days, it is clear that wood was largely used for building in early times. The one great building which has survived, a mastaba tomb, often called the Tomb of Menes, at Naqadah, shows a technique which is purely that of brick. The walls, consisting entirely of brick, are fitted externally with series of the complicated niches so familiar to us in stone technique in the false door of later times. The men who built this tomb at the dawn of the First Dynasty were not beginners but masters in the art of simple and solid building.

Of the lesser non-representative arts some have left scarcely any trace. The products of the wood-workers, for instance, and of the leather-makers, which must have been of great importance, have almost completely disappeared. On the other hand, those of the potter and the stone-vase maker have, owing to their imperishable nature, survived almost intact. The Tasian and Badarian Periods show us early stages in the making of pottery, but during the Predynastic this art came to its full perfection. The technique of preparing the clay and of firing were well under control, and the Egyptian potter was fully alive to the artistic possibilities of colour and form. A slip of hæmatite was found, when fired, to give a rich warm red colour to the vases, and by the application of a partial coat of grease before the firing it was found possible to combine this body colour with a rim of deep black. More complicated effects could be obtained by painting designs in white or red paint on a red or buff ground respectively, as described above, or perhaps best of all by incising patterns in a black biscuit and filling them with a white paste designed to show them up in greater contrast. No less attention was paid to form than to colour. Though no wheel was used the potter produced perfectly rounded vases, and the infinite variety of the forms betrays admirable feeling for line in their designers.

Still more striking are the products of the stone-vase maker. Some stones attracted him by their colours, the pink breccia for instance, others by their hardness and durability, and yet others from the polished surface which he found he could impart to them. Here the shapes are even more perfect than in pottery, and the invention of the tubular drill and the discovery of a substance, possibly emery, capable of working even the hardest diorite enabled the predynastic Egyptian to reach in this art heights which were never attained in later times (P. 94, figs. 1, 4 and 5).

One other of the lesser arts claims our notice, that of the jeweller. From the earliest times the Egyptians, with their keen eye for colour, had worn as beads the semi-precious stones, such as carnelian, amethyst, lapis lazuli, garnet and rock-crystal, and had realised the possibilities of the tasteful combination of these colours, and supplemented them by the invention of green and blue glaze. In the Predynastic Period beads had already begun to take attractive shapes instead of being mere lumps of stone, and the First Dynasty has given us very remarkable specimens of the jeweller's art in the bracelets found on the arm of a body in the tomb of Zer at Abydos (P. 95, fig. 2). Here are four bracelets which show not only considerable technical perfection, but an artist's eye for the value of colour and form. Unfortunately they stand alone, but they leave us in no doubt as to the achievement of the Egyptians of the First Dynasty in the domain of jewellery.

And so this short sketch ends. I have endeavoured to show that the love of the beautiful was already wide awake in the Egyptian of 3000 B.C. We can trace its rapid development during the Predynastic Period. We can see it casting about for new methods of expression. The noblest works of Egyptian art are undoubtedly the portrait-statues and the tomb-reliefs of the Old Kingdom. There are some of us nevertheless who

> " have loved the season
> Of Art's spring-birth so dim and dewy,"

and who see in the strivings of these early artists the promise of even greater things, which were never attained only because art fell into the deadly clutch of an unprogressive religion.

T. E. PEET

THE OLD KINGDOM

FOR the purpose of this book the first two dynasties have been excluded from the Old Kingdom and treated, as an Archaic Period, with the Predynastic Age, since their art developed immediately from that of Predynastic times and is closely connected with it. The subject of the present essay is therefore the art of the Third to the Tenth Dynasties. A certain overlapping with the early Middle Kingdom is inevitable, as from the point of view of artistic style it is difficult to say where exactly the Old Kingdom ends and the Middle Kingdom begins. Some may prefer to regard the Ninth Dynasty, for instance, as the latest phase of the Old Kingdom, others as the earliest of the Middle Kingdom. The first Intermediate Period, in which the Seventh to the Tenth Dynasties are included, is a true age of transition from one age to another. But between the Second Dynasty and the Third there is a real gap which renders it easy to begin a new age with the Third.

The First and Second Dynasties saw the crystallization of Egyptian artistic ideas and forms, under the unifying influence of a new and fixed political regime. It was then decided generally how gods and kings and the great ones of the earth should be represented plastically; the proper way of representing their figures, their clothes, their crowns, and their emblems was first arranged in a regular convention. But the settling of the convention came under the Third Dynasty; its final fixing under the Fourth.

The First Dynasty was a time of swift artistic development, especially under the vigorous rule of its earlier kings, the unifiers of the Two Lands. Under the Second the process slowed down. With the Third a new royal house of energy equal to that of the First started the growth that in two centuries produced the architectural marvels of the Gîzah Pyramids and the portrait-statues and tomb-reliefs of Sakkara.

This extraordinary development was the work of great kings, ministers, and artists. Kha'sekhemui, the first king of the dynasty, was a new Menes, a conqueror and a unifier: Zoser his son the stabilizer and conventionalizer of Egyptian civilization and art.[1] And Zoser's work was undoubtedly inspired by one man, the minister Imhotep, architect and physician, in later times deified as a god of knowledge, and identified with Asklēpios. To him Egypt owed her first great architectural triumph, the funerary temple of king Zoser, by his pyramid at Sakkara, lately excavated by Mr. C. M. Firth for the Government of H.M. King Fuad (P. 97).

[1] On the historical position of Kha'sekhemui see my " Ancient History of the Near East " (1927 edition), following E. Meyer, " Gesch. Alt."

The impression which these buildings of the Third Dynasty at Saḳḳara make is so great that it is commonly said that they can be but the culminating achievement of a long period of development. This, however, is an incorrect statement. Long and slow no doubt had been the development of Egyptian art since its beginnings in " Badarian " times, taken as a whole, but this development had proceeded by a succession of sudden jumps alternating with long periods of stagnation. One of the leaps was taken at the beginning of the dynastic period, another under the Third Dynasty itself. There is no slow period of upward development visible between the art of the First Dynasty and that of the Third. The archaic movement was followed by stagnation under the Second Dynasty ; then came the wonderful swift upward climb under the Third and Fourth that brought Egypt to the apogee of her art, in some respects, at a single bound within the space of a couple of centuries. The art of the First Dynasty, even of the beginning of the Third, is crude and irregular in comparison with the settled style of the pyramid-builders. And there were at most only two centuries between the First Dynasty and the Third. In fact, the analogy of natural evolution is false. Nature does not develop *per saltum* : man does. And he did in Egypt under the Third Dynasty, owing to the inspiration of Imhotep and his lord king Zoser.

There were no stone buildings under the First Dynasty ; even Kha'sekhemui was only the first to possess granite floors in his tomb. Tosorthros (Zoser) was said in tradition to have built the first stone house. We see it at Saḳḳara, with its pyramid, the first of these gigantic erections. And less than two hundred years later the Great Pyramid with its mathematical exactness of measure and line, its superb design and its calculated mass, rose to the sky ; and the underground temple of Kha'fra' with its colossal monoliths was excavated near by (P. 96). There is no long period of development to be seen here ; and the fact is a warning against an unthinking repetition of what is evidently very often an unjustified conclusion.

In these, the oldest stone buildings of Egypt, we see, naturally, the influence of the older methods of building in brick. The niched walls so characteristic of brick construction (as in the " Shûnat az-Zabîb " or " Flies' Barn " at Abydos, a building of the Second to the Third Dynasty), not only in Egypt but also in Babylonia (whence, indeed, the idea may have come to Egypt), are at Saḳḳara imitated in the fine white limestone of which the whole facing of the temple is built. Other walls show the influence of wood : a wooden batten construction, like that of our staithes, is simply translated into stone. And a very curious imitation, and one odd to our eyes, is that of a half-opened door in stone, that closes a colonnade. This half-opened door of stone is fixed ; it does not move. Apparently this seemed odd to the Egyptians too, for it was never imitated (P. 97).

The tall fluted pilasters or engaged columns of the chapels of the princesses Inetkais and Hetephernebti (P. 98) are definitely imitations of wooden poles, while the "fasciculated" columns of the south colonnade are clearly inspired by reed construction (P. 97). The *kheker*-ornament, ⵡⵡⵡ which appears here, represents the knotted ends of the fringe of papyrus-fronds that topped the wall of "wattle-and-daub" construction, and was itself the origin of the cavetto cornice, which does not yet appear. Stone roofs are cut in imitation of palm-logs. The whole building is a translation into the new material, stone, of motives proper to brick and wood construction of a simple type. And this fact lends probability to the view that the whole thing was the creation of one brain, that of Imhotep, who built the first stone house, and thus started Egyptian architecture on its long history of achievement in stone. And it was a sudden creation of this one brain, with no long period of special development behind it, in the course of which the characteristics of brick and wood construction would gradually have been modified and blended with new "stone" ideas. Properly speaking there are no "stone-ideas" at Saḳḳara : all is brick and wood turned into stone. The completeness and the "style" of Saḳḳara are not the result of a long development, but are the creation of one man.[2]

In the interior chambers we see minor arts brought in to reinforce the architect. The blue faience tiles of Zoser's chapel are famous (P. 98). The temple they ornament is again copied from wood-carving. The famous statue of the king shows us the art of the sculptor now coming into prominence alongside that of the architect. The grim figure (rendered grimmer by the loss of its nose, and the tearing out of its crystal eyes) is verily that of the despot god-king of the Old Kingdom, at once boon and bane to his subjects, unqualified master and lord of all. It shows the original form of the peculiar royal headdress, the nemmes, a bag to hold the hair or wig and save it from dust. In later days a more becoming form of this headdress was devised (P. 99, fig. 3).

The statue of Zoser is still somewhat archaic and crude in comparison with the work of the succeeding dynasty, but it is a great advance on the much more archaic figures of Khaʻsekhemui at Cairo and Oxford, which show peculiarities that did not survive in later times. Especially notable are the small figures incised in the pedestal of the Oxford statue, of men slain in the king's wars, with bodies and limbs contorted in their death-agonies, evidently regarded as highly picturesque by the artists of a hard and fierce age when a king and nation were in the making. We may contrast this fierce energy

[2] It is perhaps necessary for me to say, for fear of misunderstanding, that I hold this view quite independently of Prof. H. Junker, who has expressed it in his article in the " Zeitschrift für ägyptische Sprache, 1927," p. 3, and in his " Giza I," p. 73. I have held it since I visited Saqqarah in 1925 and the expression of my view will be found in my " Ancient History of the Near East " (1927 edition), Appendix, p. 593, written after my visit. I am in entire agreement with Dr. Junker on the subject.

with the orderly series of kneeling captives with their hands bound behind their backs, each representing a subdued tribe or city, all exactly alike, which take their place in the settled representations of later ages (P. 99, fig. 2).

There is a certain clumsiness still visible in private statues of the Third Dynasty. The private statue now first appears. The faithful noble and the trusted official now begin to be regarded as worthy of plastic representation as well as the king. A notable figure of the time is that of the shipbuilder Bedja, son of 'Ankhu, No. 171 in the British Museum, carried out in red granite, with an inscription in relief that still presents puzzles to the decipherer, though no longer so unintelligible as some of the inscriptions of the First Dynasty. The figure is clumsy, but the portrait is characterized; it is a real attempt at portraiture (P. 100, fig 4).

Reliefs we find frequently towards the end of the dynasty. We have one at its beginning in the relief portrait of Kha'sekhemui (? or Sanekht) at New York, which is still much in the stiff fashion of the First Dynasty carvings and the sculptured works of Wadi Magharah in Sinai, begun under King Semerkhet. But we may regard it as wishing to show what the king looked like. The love of accurate imitation of the person represented already appears (P. 99, fig. 1).

In the tomb of Neferma'at at Mêdûm we see an attempt, not wholly successful, at representation on the flat wall by means of inlaid colour. The reliefs of the late Third and the Fourth Dynasty tombs at Gîzah follow, with their multitudinous pictures of men and animals carrying out the labour of the farms for their dead lords.

And then in the round we reach the consummate portraiture of the kings Kha'fra' and Menkaura', in which the sculptor also has produced masterpieces, and of private persons like Ra'hetep and his wife Nofret, to whose images the painter has added the colours of life, and the cunning artificer has given by means of crystal eyeball and metal iris a lifelike reproduction of the human eye that has never been surpassed (Pp. 101-103).

Yet the figures are still clumsy, at any rate when seated; feet and hands are roughly blocked out. It was the face alone that really mattered. When Kha'fra' (presumably) fashioned the Great Sphinx of Gîzah as his image, it was his face only that mattered. That must be like. The rest of the body might equally well be a lion's or a man's; and for the purpose of expressing the power and ferocity of kingship it was best to make him a lion-sphinx.

The attitudes were fixed by convention that now became universal. They were rooted in the old archaic art of the First Dynasty, when artists could only represent figures in the round in certain clumsy and wooden attitudes. These attitudes were fixed, they could be improved upon and refined, and were so, already under the Fourth Dynasty, but no great variation of them was possible till the free time of the later Eighteenth Dynasty. The Egyptian of the Fourth Dynasty did not take the final step that brought the Greek from the stiff *xoana* and Victor and Apollo figures of the seventh and sixth centuries to the freedom of the Parthenon frieze in the fifth. It was as if the Greeks of the fifth century had developed the portrait-heads of the sixth century sculpture while the figures belonging to them remained in the stiff attitudes of the seventh and sixth somewhat refined, but still the same.

The reason for this arrest of development is usually given as " religious." What was the reason for this sculpture at all ? Greek sculpture was religious in origin. It was votive, and the Egyptian also was now partly so, in later times much more so. But the main reason for the making of the portrait figures of kings and men and of all the tomb-reliefs was the not wholly " religious " one of preserving the dead man " alive " in the tomb with all his ordinary life and surroundings about him. The Egyptians " loved life and hated death " : they wanted to believe that by representing the dead as alive, and by preserving his body, they did assure him a continuance of life in the world of the tomb. Hence the necessity of real and accurate portraiture of the head and face, while feet and hands and body did not matter so much. They would be represented as they had been before, especially since a really religious convention had under the First Dynasty prescribed how kings and gods should be depicted, so that men also, now first represented in honour, could be conventionally shown. But you must make the statue, intended to be placed in the tomb, " like " in face. And the habit of careful portraiture, thus originating, became ingrained in Egyptian art, only failing in degenerate times and places. To it we owe the magnificent portraits of the Old and Middle Kingdoms.

To the period of the Fourth and Fifth Dynasties belong some of the chief treasures of Cairo and Paris, Ra'hetep and Nofret, the Sheikh el-Beled, Kha'fra' seated, Menkaura' and his wife, Menkaura' with the goddesses of the Nomes, Ra'nofer, Ti, and Hemôn at Cairo ; Kake and the *Scribe accroupi* at Paris ; while at London, Nenkheftka and the beautiful little alabaster statue of a girl (presumably a princess ; she is rather too precious to be a mere serving-maid) are worthy representatives of this art (Pp. 104-110).

A most interesting and important point in connection with these Old Kingdom portraits is their facial type which seems extraordinarily European. This is specially noticeable in some of the " reserve heads " for the use of the dead man (in case his chief statue lost its head) in the tombs. The type is often so northern that we are disposed to think that the " dynastic Egyptian " invaders from Syria, who started the great development of culture in predynastic times, really came originally from much farther north than Syria: that in fact they had come ultimately from Europe, and were the oldest forerunners of the Aryans, the first, perhaps, of the great overflows of Central European population into the East and South.

Passing on to another material we find, under the Sixth Dynasty, copper used with effect on the grand scale in the figures of Pepi I and his son, found at Kôm al-aḥmar (Hierakonpolis), and now at Cairo (P. 108). The bodies must have been hammered, but the question whether the faces, or at any rate that of the boy, were cast, is one that demands solution. In the analogous and earlier copper-work of al-'Ubaid in Babylonia, we find the heads of some of the smaller bull or heifer figures cast, without doubt. The adoption of the casting process marks a great step forward in the use of metal in art, and we would like to fix if possible the approximate date of its invention.

The Pepi statues were not the most ancient of their kind in Egypt. The Palermo stone records the making of a copper statue for Kha'sekhemui (beginning of the Third Dynasty). And the fact of the record is proof that the thing was considered of great importance at the time : it was no doubt the first metal statue made in Egypt. We may compare the legend of the building of the first stone house by Tosorthros.

Many of the statues of the Old Kingdom were in wood. These were often large under the Fifth Dynasty, but under the Sixth became smaller, and are placed in the tomb with models of workmen and female slaves at work baking bread, ploughing or carrying burdens for their dead lords. Later on, under the Eleventh Dynasty, these developed into elaborate models, often with sailed boats with rowers, besides the model figures of workmen. Many of the Sixth Dynasty figures of the lords, standing with their staves in their hands, are beautifully carved, notably that of a certain Meria'-Hashetef, from Sedment, in the British Museum, found by Prof. Petrie and given by the National Art Collections' Fund. The engaging twist of the body in the figure, however, is not due to art or intended by the artist, but to a natural warping of the wood in the course of centuries. The Egypian convention did not allow of such free attitudes as this at any time in sculpture, hardly even in the 'Amarna period, though we do not know what might have happened had that short period of freedom persisted (Pp. 109-112).

If the Egyptians laid stress on human portraiture, so did they also on that of the beasts. No finer representations of animals exist than those of the Egyptian artists of the Fourth and Fifth Dynasties. The donkeys from Gîzah at Berlin and Leiden (P. 114), the famous geese of Mêdûm at Cairo, are veritable triumphs of keen observation and trained mimetic power. In them we do not see the abandonment of non-essentials, like the feet and hands of man ; for no religious or semi-religious reason obliged the artist to concentrate attention on the head. The mimetic power of the sculptor, sharpened by the necessity of making faithful portraits of men, naturally reproduced animal forms of beauty without difficulty. They too became more or less fixed in style. So far as gods and men were concerned, the Egyptian had already, but for the variation of the portrait, got into the state of mind of the Byzantine painter, who could only represent God and the Theotokos and the Child or the Saints in a certain way in accordance with the rules of the Ἑρμηνεῖα or " Guide " for Ecclesiastical Painters. There was a right and proper way to represent people, as we see from the stele of the painter Irtisen, under the Eleventh Dynasty, who tells us that he well knew how to portray the " forms of going forth and returning, the poising of the arm to bring the hippopotamus low, the going of the runner." And there became a right way of depicting animals also, in which however there was perhaps more scope for individual variation than in the case of gods and men. The portrait was always accurate ; and so Egyptian representations of birds, insects, and plants are always apt to remind us of the meticulously drawn and coloured illustrations in manuals of zoology or botany. In Minoan art, however, it may be difficult to distinguish between a lily and a butterfly. The Cretans were poets as well as temperamental artists : the Egyptians were supreme mimetic art-workers, steady and solid in achievement as their own pyramids. Egyptian art was simply mimetic. Ideas of veiled mystery were as foreign to it as in reality to Egyptian religion and life, originally, however rife charlatanry may have been in late times. Khaʿfraʿʾs sphinx was no Bodhisattva. There is no mystic brooding on eternity in the intention of Egyptian colossi, which were just big official portrait-statues and nothing more, as the Pyramids were just big tombs and nothing more. We see the prototype of the colossi in the statues of Zoser and of Khaʿfraʿ. We are indeed apt to read into Egyptian civilization and art much that never was there. It is the limitations of Egyptian art, fixed under the Old Kingdom, that have given rise to these misconceptions. We see that Egyptian art can be absurd, as in its convention, in the flat, of the upper part of the body being in full-face, while face and lower part are in profile. This was fixed now, though one or two artists of the Old Kingdom tried to devise some truer method, with disastrous results, as we may see from the reliefs of Neferseshem-Ptah at Saḳḳara (P. 114), published by Capart.[3] They gave up trying to get this right, and now the convention imposes itself upon us, and does not seem so absurd as it is. So also in the hieratic-looking figure, considered mysterious and Buddha-like ; though the treatment of hands and feet is not absurd, it is formal.

The architecture of temples and tombs, starting in the development of stone-using by Zoser and Imhotep, assumed a new form under the Fourth and Fifth Dynasties, when the classical orders of Egyptian columns arose in lily and papyrus form, and temples took on themselves their well-known style with reliefs of kings and gods on their walls. The origin in wood and brick work of the stone architecture is still evident, but a true development, not a sudden change, had operated and forms are used more appropriate to stone itself, developed, but not mere translations, from wood and brick.

[3] " Une Rue de Tombeaux à Saqqarah " ; Brussels, 1907.

Many Egyptian temple-columns that now bear the name of Rameses II, or any other confirmed usurper of the work of others, were originally made under the Old Kingdom, and so bear no advertisement on them of the name of their maker. The kings of the Old Kingdom did not advertise. The Great Pyramid would have been the biggest advertisement any Egyptian king could have had. But Khufu did not " sign " it. It is remarkable that Rameses did not usurp it ! The work of the Pyramid-Builders and of the Old Kingdom was, however, not to the taste of the Ramessides. It was not till the bankruptcy of the " Empire " and disappearance of imperial pomp that the Memphites and Saites went back to the purer taste of the older day, and in their archaistic sculpture imitated the old work so well that, nowadays, but for the inscriptions we should hardly be able to tell an archaistic work of the Twenty-Sixth Dynasty from an original of the Fifth.

So far as small art is concerned we have not so much material as in later days. The tomb of queen Hetepheres, however, has shown us that the combination of wood and gold overlay for furniture was as well known as in the time of Tutankhamen (Pp. 116-117); and we can be assured that the jewellery of gold, electrum and semi-precious stones, so characteristic of the Twelfth Dynasty, was not without its parallel in earlier days, though only rare examples of it are likely to survive. The jewellery of the First Dynasty already shows motives that survived through the Old Kingdom into the later art. Amulets and beads of carnelian and other stones were well known, and little amuletic figures of gods and holy animals, strung as beads, and such amulets as the human leg and foot in carnelian, are characteristic of the Sixth Dynasty ; while the scarab-seal in glazed faience or steatite was beginning to make its appearance, its predecessor the " button-seal " being typical of the end of the Old Kingdom. The cylinder-seal was still used generally, but died out of use in the succeeding age (Pp. 120-121).

Faience is generally of the light blue colour characteristic of the First Dynasty, but a deeper blue begins to appear under the Sixth, and combines with a black haematite glaze to form the characteristic dark blue faience with black decoration of the Middle Kingdom. Vases of Old Kingdom faience are rare. But of the ordinary pottery, naturally, a great deal has been found. That of the archaic age is generally poor in comparison with the magnificent Predynastic ceramic, but under the Third Dynasty, contemporaneously with the revival in greater art, a fine red polished ware began to appear which is characteristic of the Fourth-Sixth Dynasties, and often shows skilled and graceful forms (P. 119).

Though pottery had degenerated, the art of making stone vases had continued undegenerate. Some of the finest stone vases we know, of a translucent diorite, date from the Third-Fourth Dynasty, and the lovely alabasters of the Sixth are well known (Pp. 118-119).

Sculpture then is the outstanding manifestation of the Egyptian artistic genius under the Old Kingdom, and it is dominated by the desire for accurate portraiture, which laid the foundation of the mimetic tradition that shows itself throughout ancient Egyptian art. At the same time a wonderful individual brain created in a few years with a Merlin's wand a world of magnificent architecture in a material not previously used on a grand scale, stone. This, though its style was not immediately followed, yet by the fact of its existence inspired the architects of the Pyramid-builders to use combinations which were the foundation of Ancient Egyptian architecture as we know it. The sacred torch was handed down to successive generations of " men and the sons of men," and the Ptolemaic temple of Edfu in the third century B.C. is the lineal descendant of the fanes that were erected by the pharaohs of the Old Kingdom 2,500 years before. This extraordinary progress in a few years could not have been effected without the driving power of despotic monarchs, bent on carrying out their intelligent will. The rulers of Egypt, kings and their nobles, had brought to the Nile-land from the north brains more powerful than those of the indigenous Nilotes ; we see the result in the sudden development of Egyptian culture under the Old Kingdom. And the Egyptian King of the oldest dynasties had unlimited power over his subjects : we see this in the literary references to the dooming power of " the god " (i.e., the king) in the " Teachings " of the time, and in the fact of the great Pyramids : " what the god doeth is unknown." But long and weak reigns were to give the opportunity to local nobles to develop their more " feudal " power, independent of the monarchy; division and intestinal war brought the magnificent civilization and art of the Old Kingdom to an end ; foreigners invaded the land from North and South ; art became inconceivably debased. The decadence of the age is seen in the gloomy vaticinations of the " prophet " Ipuwer, who refers sarcastically to the weakness of the ruler, asks whither the ship of State is being steered amid a sea of troubles, and can only express the hope that one day better times will evolve, and a Messianic ruler revive the glories of the past. This hope was fulfilled by the kings of the Eleventh and Twelfth Dynasties. But the great Middle Kingdom revival of civilization and art too had its day, to be followed by another period of decadence and anarchy equally reflected in the arts, followed by revival again, and so on till the end of the story. The unquenchable life of the Nile-folk always remains, the inspiration of its art never dies. The generations of men pass away ; the spirit bides.

H. R. HALL

THE HERAKLEOPOLITAN PERIOD
AND THE MIDDLE KINGDOM

ONLY a few examples of statues and reliefs in stone that can be dated to the Herakleopolitan Period have survived to the present day, and few deserve serious attention as works of art. During this period wooden models replaced the tomb-chapel reliefs except in rare instances, and wooden statuettes, often quite small and of inferior workmanship, were substituted for the fine portrait statues so frequently found in the Old Kingdom mastabehs at Gizeh and elsewhere. On the other hand, a certain number of wooden statuettes of remarkable quality that may possibly be assigned to this epoch still survive, such as the famous ebony statuette shown on P. 139. An example of the rare stone statuettes of the Herakleopolitan Period is that in alabaster of Mesekhti (P. 123) found in his tomb at Asyût and probably to be assigned to the Tenth Dynasty. The sculptor has broken away entirely from all the established rules of Egyptian art. The legs sprawl apart in front of the seat and the arms and hands lie limply along the thighs and knees. The dignity and beautiful proportions of the Old Kingdom are sadly missing. Ugly though this statue is, however, its vitality and freedom of pose deserve notice, and devotees of " modern art " may find much to like in it !

With the Eleventh Dynasty stone statuettes and reliefs become more frequent, but those dating from the earlier half of the dynasty are usually very crude,[1] the statuettes being as ungainly, though not as vigorous, as that of Mesekhti.

The re-establishment of a strong central government towards the end of the Dynasty, and the consequent unified control of public works, resulted in the revival of the old artistic standards. This is to be seen in the somewhat heavy and coarse-featured painted sandstone statue of Menthotpe III (P. 122). The work is strong and the parts hold together, a grateful relief from the loose treatment of such statues as that of Mesekhti.

Some of the finest royal statues of the Twelfth Dynasty have been found in Lower Egypt, where flourished a school of sculptors with a distinctive style of their own. Their work possesses an almost brutal vigour, as though there flowed in the veins of these artists some of the blood of the fierce Asiatic invaders who had overrun the eastern part of the Delta after the collapse of the Sixth Dynasty. It will be observed that these Northern sculptors sought not only to reproduce the outward features, but to suggest also the inward qualities of the persons portrayed. Earlier examples of their work are the black granite statues of Amenemhēt I, Senusret I and Nofret, the

[1] An exception is the beautiful stela of Thethi in the British Museum (No. 614).

wife of Senusret II (Pp. 124-126), the first and last found at Tanis, the other at Alexandria.

Markedly different from them are the famous limestone statues of Senusret I, found in his pyramid at Lisht and doubtless the products of an Upper or Middle Egyptian workshop (P. 127). These statues are of the finest workmanship, but of forcefulness and strength they have none. These doll-like figures sit primly, almost unsteadily, on their thrones, and one somehow has the impression that the sculptors who fashioned them were trained in a school more accustomed to work in wood than in stone. This may well have been the case, for the wooden models and statues referred to at the beginning of the chapter are the outstanding features of the art of the preceding period.

Certain portraits of Senusret II and Amenemḥēt III rank among the noblest products of Egyptian art. Though some have been found in Upper Egypt and a few are of unknown provenance, the fact that others come from Tanis and elsewhere in the Delta, and that all alike are characterised by an astounding vigour, sometimes amounting to ferocity, suggests that they are productions of the Northern School. The Delta sculptors of the latter half of the Twelfth Dynasty far surpassed their predecessors, who worked for Amenemḥēt I and Senusret I, both in ability to express a likeness—the faces of the statues are clearly actual portraits—and in their technique, which is sometimes of unsurpassed delicacy.

A fine example is the black granite statue of Senusret III (P. 128), found by the Egypt Exploration Society at Dêr el-Baḥri. This is a very noble work. Senusret looks every inch a ruler, but also a man who has drunk deeply of experience and knows the vanity of human greatness. Almost as fine is the head of the same king found in 1926 at Medamūt (P. 130). Two other magnificent examples are the sphinx with the face of Amenemḥēt III from Tanis, and a torso of the same Pharaoh wearing an enormous wig (Pp. 131 and 132, fig. 2).

But perhaps the most striking of them all are two heads, also portraits of Amenemḥēt III, one well under life size depicting him in the prime of life (P. 133), and the other, measuring only 130 mm. from the top of the head to the chin, representing him as elderly (P. 129). It is hardly an exaggeration to say that they are two of the greatest works of art that have come down to us from the ancient world. Not quite equal to them in beauty, though well worth showing, is the head of the god Amūn (P. 132, fig. 1). The sculptor has clearly given the god the features of Amenemḥēt III, from whose reign the statue dates.

To the statues we have just discussed that of Amenemḥēt III from Hawāra presents a marked contrast. It is pleasing and of fine workmanship, but is lacking in strength and forcefulness (P. 134).

A certain number of royal statues of the Thirteenth Dynasty survive, but, though some of them are imposing, they are heavy and uninspired and do not deserve a place in this book.

Among the Middle Kingdom statues and statuettes of private persons there are to be found no such masterpieces as the statue of the famous " Sheikh el-Beled," or those of Reʿ-ḥotpe and Nofret, Reʿ-nofer, and the seated scribe in the Louvre, but there are some of considerable merit. Good examples are the very gracious portrait of the Lady Sennuy; the statues of a seated man wrapped in a cloak, and of a standing man similarly cloaked—two most dignified figures; the statuettes of Amenemhēteʿonkh and Ptah-em-saf-senebtify; and the small statue of Antef son of Sebekunnu (Pp. 135 and 136). The two Eleventh Dynasty statuettes of Meri (P. 137, fig. 1) are of excellent technique and are perhaps interesting enough to be reproduced here.

Wood was employed for statues and statuettes at all times in Ancient Egypt, though more particularly, so it would seem, during the Herakleopolitan Period. Attention has already been drawn to the remarkable Herakleopolitan wooden statuette on P. 139. Two fine examples dating from the Middle Kingdom are the statuette of Senusret I and the statue of the ka, or guardian spirit, of King Horus, the latter a masterly study in the nude (P. 138).

Most museums contain examples of the painted wooden models which were first placed in the tombs during the Sixth Dynasty, almost completely supplanted the reliefs in the tomb-chapels during the Herakleopolitan Period, and were still buried with the dead in the Eleventh and possibly in the Twelfth Dynasty. These models depict in a vivid manner the scenes and objects of daily life—a house and garden, a musical party, male and female servants plying their tasks in kitchen, bakery, brewery, and butchery, peasants working in farm-yard or field artisans in the workshops, fishermen catching fish, boats sailing or being rowed on the river (Pp. 139-141).

The majority of the models, though nearly always entertaining and instructive, are crude and of little artistic merit. However, the latter charge cannot be brought against the two splendidly carved and lifelike companies of soldiers, the one heavy armed infantry and the other archers (P. 140), found in the tomb of Mesekhti (see P. 123) at Asyût, and so dating from the Herakleopolitan Period. Of the same date, probably, is the admirable statuette of a woman carrying a basket on her head (P. 137, fig. 2), and the figure of a cook (P. 139, fig. 2) fanning a brazier, over which he is roasting a duck (now broken off) on a spit. The finest and most interesting collection of models known to us was discovered a few years ago in the tomb of an important Theban official of the Eleventh Dynasty, named Meketrēʿ. Examples of these are shown on Pp. 140 and 141. As a rule, even the best reliefs of the Eleventh and Twelfth Dynasties (P. 142, figs. 1 and 2) are more remarkable for their beautiful finish than for their originality and liveliness, in which respect they fall behind those of the Old Kingdom. Notable exceptions to this criticism occur, however, in two tomb-chapels at Mêr. The naturalistic treatment of many of the figures in these reliefs is hardly paralleled elsewhere in Egypt. Especially deserving of mention are the splendid hunting scene (Fig. 2), the fighting bulls and the lassoing of an ox (Fig. 3), in the tomb-chapel of Senbi, and the blind singer and harpist, the coarse-featured papyrus harvesters, the fat old men talking to a boat builder, and the emaciated Bishāri herdsman, in the tomb-chapel of Senbi's son Ukhhotpe (Pp. 143 and 144).

The magnificently painted wooden coffins of the Herakleopolitan Period (P. 144) suggest that frescoes of great beauty may have been executed by the artists of those days. If that were so, none unhappily have survived, or anyhow yet come to light.

Fig. 2. The Lord Senbi shooting big game in the desert. The animals have been driven into an enclosure.
From A. M. Blackman "The Rock Tombs of Meir," I, Pl. vi

Fig. 3. Two bulls fighting and an ox being roped.
From A. M. Blackman "The Rock Tombs of Meir," I, Pl. xi

The tomb-chapels at Beni-Hasan supply us with a large number of wall-paintings of the Eleventh and Twelfth Dynasties, most of great archæological interest and some of great merit. Good work is also to be found in the frescoed tomb-chapel of Antefōker, the vizier of Senusret I, an example being the vigorously rendered dancing girls (P. 145). Two of the best paintings at Beni-Hasan are in the Twelfth Dynasty tomb-chapel of Khnemḥotpe, the one depicting an acacia tree with birds perched on its branches (Frontispiece), and the other two farm-hands attending to a couple of oryxes (P. 145). It will be observed that the painter of the latter picture has attempted to show the shoulders of the standing man in profile, and not twisted round full face according to the usual Egyptian convention.

From what has survived, we can see that the funerary furniture of the wealthier and official classes during the Herakleopolitan Period and the Middle Kingdom was often of the finest description. Though the decoration of the wooden coffins, so elaborate during the Herakleopolitan Period, became much simpler early in the Twelfth Dynasty, the craftsmanship of the tomb-furnishers shows no signs of deterioration. How admirable this was is well illustrated in the alabaster jars for the embalmed viscera (commonly called " Canopic jars ") with their stoppers in the shape of human heads, and the wooden chest in which they were placed, shown on P. 141. These particular objects, which were found at El-Bersheh, possibly date from the Tenth or Eleventh Dynasty, but may well be as late as the Twelfth.

A. M. BLACKMAN

ARCHITECTURE AND THE MINOR ARTS

WHILE the First Intermediate Period and the Middle Kingdom have left us comparatively few examples of statuary and relief, they are fortunately represented by a considerable wealth of smaller artistic objects. The desire to decorate the things used in everyday life, to be surrounded with what was pretty or quaint, already visible in the Predynastic Period, was never more effectively expressed than under the Twelfth Dynasty, and at no period were the Egyptian craftsmen more completely masters of their material. We may take it for granted, for instance, that the kings of the Twelfth Dynasty were surrounded in their palaces with the same wealth of elaborate furniture as the royal persons of the Eighteenth, Yuia and Tuyu and Tutankhamun; though, to judge by those categories of objects in which comparison is possible, the earlier products were probably on the whole in far better taste. These palaces, however, have long since disappeared, and nothing but a lucky tomb-find will enable us to put this to the test. That the furniture of this epoch was in the main similar in design to that of the New Empire, however, is clear from the many representations of it which occur in the reliefs and paintings in the tombs.

The art of pottery-making had never recovered from the blow dealt to it in the Late Predynastic Period by the introduction of the more decorative kinds of stone for the making of the finer vases. Throughout the Old Kingdom it degenerated, if degeneration was possible, and the Twelfth Dynasty did nothing to revive it; indeed it has to be confessed that the only tolerable pottery found in this period consists of the black flasks with white-filled incised patterns from Syria, and the lovely bell-shaped cups of thin red ware with black top which occasionally wandered in from the Sudan. On the other hand, the art of making stone vases was not lost. That there is no longer the variety or the number found in the earlier dynasties is perhaps a mere accident, for the technique is hardly less perfect, and the designs are as beautiful as ever. Alabaster is still a favourite material (P. 149, fig. 1), though there now vies with it the equally beautiful grey-blue marble, which, however, is used mainly for small vases such as kohl-pots. With these occur grey serpentine, and—though very rarely—obsidian (P. 149, fig. 2); there is distinctly less readiness than in the Old Kingdom to work in the more resistant materials, such as diorite. In the matter of shapes, the slender pointed alabasters of the Sixth Dynasty have gone, to be replaced, however, by almost equally beautiful vases of globular shape; the tumbler-shaped vase—the so-called Pepi-jar—is still a favourite.

In the smaller forms of art, however, the chief glory of the Middle Kingdom is its jewellery. Here we see a technical skill which in some respects has never been surpassed combined with an almost impeccable taste in design and an inexhaustible fund of decorative inventiveness. We know next to nothing about the jewellery of the Old Kingdom, but it is difficult to believe that it was finer than that of the Twelfth Dynasty; and the superiority of the latter to that of the New Empire will have escaped no one who has compared the Middle Kingdom jewellery of the old Jewel Room at Cairo with that of Tutankhamun. Lucky finds by de Morgan at Dahshur and Petrie at Illahûn have brought into our museums the contents of the jewel-cases of several noble ladies of the Twelfth Dynasty. The technique of this jewellery comprises, in addition to the usual casting, chasing and engraving of gold and silver, the arts of granulating by means of minute beads of metal, either fused or soldered into position (P. 148), and of inlaying on a gold base flat slips of various semi-precious stones (cloisonné-work). Recent investigations have shown that the inlays are at this period all natural stones, and never glass. The most striking of these jewels are perhaps the pectorals bearing the cartouches of various Twelfth Dynasty kings. In these the beauty of the inlaid technique with its variety of colours is enhanced by the open-work design, and one is at a loss to know which to admire most, the more solid and highly coloured pectoral of Amenemḥēt III (P. 147, fig. 3), or the lighter and more delicate one of Senusret II (P. 147, fig. 1), which shows just as careful finishing on the plain gold back as on the face. Equally beautiful are the three crowns. That of Sat-ḥatḥor-iunut (P. 147, fig. 2) is a plain broad band of burnished gold with streamers on three sides and a double plume of thin sheet-gold at the back. In front is a royal cobra in open-work, inlaid with carnelian and lapis lazuli, and round the gold band are riveted fifteen rosettes. One of Khnemit's coronets (P. 146, fig. 2) is more elaborate in style than this, but no less lovely with its ingenious design and wealth of brightly coloured inlay ; the other will to some appear the most perfect of all, for it is a simple unaffected copy of a wreath of small flowers with, for sole decoration, a Maltese cross in the front (P. 146, fig. 1).

It would take far too long to describe at any length the smaller jewels, and it must suffice to refer the reader to P. 148, begging him to notice both the admirable technique and the wide field from which the designs are drawn—butterflies, shells, stars, birds—as well as the able combination of these with purely geometrical designs. In addition to gold and silver, the materials mainly used are the semi-precious stones, lapis lazuli, carnelian, amethyst, garnet and green felspar, this last very typical of this particular period.

While dealing with jewellery we must not overlook the various types of seal which were so often worn on the person, and, in the case of scarabs, frequently mounted in the bezel of a gold ring. The Old Kingdom seal in the form of a cylinder used for rolling on damp clay still survived under the Twelfth Dynasty and we have some good examples in glazed steatite (P. 121). During the First Intermediate Period the scarab seal had come into use, perhaps as a derivative of the button seal (Pp. 121 and 150). The scarabs of the Middle Kingdom are among the largest and best which the Egyptian lapidaries ever produced. The different parts of the beetle itself are very accurately rendered, and the name of the king or official on the base is finely cut and in some cases surrounded by a well-designed border, generally of spiral volutes. Scarabs were even made in such hard materials as carnelian and amethyst, but these were seldom inscribed ; the more usual substance was steatite, which was covered with a glaze unsurpassed at any other period for colour and brilliance.

This technique of glazing was not confined to such small objects as scarabs and cylinder-seals. Some of the finest examples of glazed bowls (faience) date from the Middle Kingdom, and even more remarkable are the figures of animals to which this art was applied. P. 151 (fig. 1) shows one of the finest of these, a hippopotamus with head thrown back and mouth wide open, an admirably naturalistic piece of moulding. P. 150 contains other equally successful products of the same art.

The architectural achievements of the Middle Kingdom are almost a closed book to us. The temples and palaces which the monarchs of the Twelfth Dynasty built were entirely swept away by their successors, and we can only replace them in imagination from the scanty vestiges which remain. Our knowledge of the private house of the period is based—apart from the models in Meketrē's tomb—solely on the town of the workmen who built the pyramid of Senusret II at Illahûn, and it would hardly be safe to regard its very temporary architecture as typical of the best Middle Kingdom work.

While the dwellings of kings and men have thus perished their tombs have survived in large numbers. The typical royal tomb was a rock-chamber surmounted by a pyramid, but the latter is no longer, as in the Old Kingdom, built of imperishable stone, but of mere sun-dried brick, owing, perhaps, not so much to diminution of power as to the prevalence of sounder and less wasteful economic principles. An exception to this choice of the cheaper and more easily handled material is to be seen in the pyramid-tomb of King Menthotpe III at Dêr el-Baḥri, of which a restoration is shown on P. 152 (fig. 2). The style and execution of this building show that in architecture Egypt had made a rapid recovery from the disasters of the First Intermediate Period; it is an earnest of better things to come, things, however, which unfortunately have not survived for us.

The nobles of the period were buried, when suitable cliffs presented themselves, in tombs hewn out of the solid rock. The best known of these tombs are those of Beni-Ḥasan. P. 152 (fig. 1) shows the exterior of the tomb of Khnemḥotpe II, a colonnaded façade with a central doorway. The "Doric" columns were until recently thought to be the earliest of this type in Egypt; we now know that very similar columns, though not free-standing, were in use at Saḳḳara as early as the Third Dynasty. In the interior of the tomb of Amenemḥēt are columns of the same kind; the reproduction in the solid rock of the architraves and vaulting of an ordinary stone-built chamber is especially worthy of note.

T. E. PEET

THE NEW KINGDOM

ON his return to Athens from a visit to the Nile Valley Plato laid stress on what he called the "conservatism" of Egyptian Art, remarking that it was not lawful either for the Egyptian painters, or "others who work out forms," to introduce any novelty. "By observing," he says, "you will discover that the paintings and sculptures of the Nile Valley executed millenniums ago are neither more beautiful nor more ugly than those turned out of hand at the present day, but are worked off according to the same art." That this criticism is entirely untrue is now generally admitted, but no period in the history of Egyptian Art is better fitted to refute it than the one treated in the present section. More monuments have survived of this period—called the "New Kingdom"—than of any other. Apart from the magnificent series of objects from the tomb of Tutankhamen, our excavators have, within the last half-century, brought to light many of the choicest heirlooms bequeathed to us by antiquity. Their recovery has added so greatly to the world's artistic wealth and knowledge that it is now as easy for the trained eye to assign a statue or statuette to a Pharaoh's reign as it is for the student of Greek art to assign a Greek sculpture to the school of Pheidias, Praxiteles or Lysippus. The same is true of other objects of Egyptian art; a faience bowl or chalice, a piece of jewellery, a chair or a decorated box, can now, without hesitation, be dated to within a few years. To speak of the "conservatism" of Egyptian art is no longer possible.

But the accurate dating of objects is only the first step forward, and we are very far from understanding much in the history of the art of the New Kingdom. There is, of course, continuity in its history from the period which immediately preceded it, but many new motifs appear, and there is new treatment of old motifs, but whether this is due to foreign influence we do not know. Historical problems are involved whose existence we are only beginning to realise. Every day the whole subject of the ancient civilisation of the Nile Valley and Delta is becoming more complicated; everywhere there is a tangling of threads rather than an unravelling of them.

Most of the surviving temples that were erected in the Nile Valley belong to the New Kingdom. Those at Heliopolis and Memphis have disappeared, but at Thebes it is still possible for us to wander through the colonnaded halls and corridors of several of the most stupendous creations of the Egyptian architects. At Luxor there is the temple of Amenhotep III (P. 153), which was enlarged by Rameses II; the latter Pharaoh placed between the columns of one of his halls colossal statues of himself with his Consort (P. 154). At Karnak are the temples of the various Theban deities, including the great one of Amen, which, begun in the Middle Kingdom, was added to by many of the monarchs of the eighteenth and later dynasties until it became the greatest temple in the world. Here we see for the first time in history those huge towers of masonry—called "pylons"—flanking the entrance-door of the temple which are so characteristic of Egyptian architecture. These massive structures were—as their ornamentation of lashed reeds down their edges and below their cavetto cornices clearly proves—but copies in stone of earlier constructions in wattle-and-daub, the common building material that was employed in the Delta. Before them the kings of the New Kingdom erected enormous statues of themselves, some of which remain in place. The famous Colossi on the Plain of Thebes were the pair Amenhotep III erected before the entrance of his Mortuary Temple, but the pylon behind them has disappeared. In front of the portals were also the great flagstaves with their long streamers that fluttered in the wind ; they were fastened at the foot in the masonry of the pylon and higher up by metal clamps. These flagstaves, of cypress or fir imported from the Lebanon, are the survivals of the primitive flagposts originally used for marking out sacred ground. Another feature of temple architecture of the New Kingdom was the Hypostyle Hall ; some were immense structures, that of Seti I (P. 155) at Karnak is divided into three aisles with roof resting upon one hundred and thirty-four huge columns which are arranged in sixteen rows, of which the two central ones are higher than the others. This imposing hall of Seti I ranks among the wonders of the world and covers an area of 5,450 square yards.

Across the river at Thebes, along the edge of the Libyan desert, were the Mortuary Temples of the monarchs of the New Kingdom. At Der el Bahari is that of Hatshepsut (P. 156), which, in plan and conception, is different from all others in Egypt. It is built in three tiers or terraces with a central ramp sloping upwards to a sanctuary cut in the limestone cliff at the back of the sacred edifice. It was never finished, but it has not suffered greatly at the hands of time. On its northern side is a colonnade of sixteen-sided columns and a small chapel dedicated to the jackal-headed deity Anubis (P. 152, fig. 3), decorated with painted scenes which are as fresh as when they left the painter's brush. The natural setting of this monument of Egypt's famous queen is one of the most beautiful that can be imagined. The architect who designed it, by name Senenmut, was privileged to excavate his own tomb in the living rock far below its floor. The shrine which contains the Hathor Cow protecting the young king Amenhotep II, and which is now in the Cairo museum (P. 157), was found at the back of the uppermost terrace of the temple. The Hathor Cow is one of the greatest achievements in animal sculpture that have come down to us from antiquity.

Another Mortuary Temple, but of a different type from that of Hatshepsut, is the one at Medinet Habu at Thebes, which was erected by Rameses III. This building was planned like the temples on the eastern bank of the river that were erected for the worship of the gods. Here we see the massive pylons, large courts, and a Hypostyle Hall, with many smaller chambers. The first court is flanked on right and left by roofed colonnades; on the south side the columns have calyx capitals; on the north side they are square pillars against which stand colossal statues of the king as Osiris. Approached by an inclined plane is the second pylon, giving entrance to the second colonnaded court, which has a raised platform at the end. Beyond is the Hypostyle Hall, the roof of which, now fallen, was supported by twenty-four columns in four rows of six. Beyond again are more columned chambers and rooms dedicated to various deities, while on either side of the Hypostyle Hall are rooms which served as storehouses for the temple treasures.

The palaces of the Pharaohs and the dwelling-houses of the Nobles were much lighter structures than the temples; for the most part they were built of unbaked brick and wood. Nearly all have disappeared, but near Medinet Habu can still be seen the lower courses of the walls of Amenhotep III's palace, while at El Amarna are preserved the lower parts of the walls of the palaces of members of the Royal Family and of great officials. The ceilings, walls, and floors of the rooms were gaily decorated with paintings. In the Theban palace were found many fallen ceilings painted with designs of pigeons, pin-tailed ducks, and butterflies flying across the blue sky. Geometrical and spiral designs also appear here. Similar ceiling patterns are to be seen in many of the Theban tombs. At El Amarna the floors of the palaces were plastered and painted, the designs representing gardens full of flowering plants, or lotus pools with birds and fish, bordered by reeds and other plants, while calves skip amongst the vegetation. Of mural paintings some were found in Amenhotep III's palace, but the most important that have survived are two from El Amarna. One of these was discovered by Sir Flinders Petrie in 1892 and depicts Ikhnaton with his queen and their daughters. Two of the young princesses are seated on cushions and are playing together by their mother's side; they are both nude and are drawn with astonishing skill. This mural painting, now in the Ashmolean Museum, is the prettiest work from an ancient Egyptian's brush that has come down to us. An artist's sketch on a limestone slab shows a charming study of one of Ikhnaton's daughters seated on a cushion and eating a bird (P. 163). The second mural painting, discovered only a few years ago, represents a plantation of papyrus reeds among which blue rock-pigeons, turtle-doves and a pied kingfisher are flying. Around the plantation are beds of flowers delineated with great accuracy. The paintings were continuous around the room; a parallel to this wonderful work of art is in the Villa Livia near Rome, where all four walls of a room are painted with a garden scene. No verbal account of the artistic qualities and colour of these two specimens of Egyptian wall-painting could accurately reproduce them to the mind's eye and it is fortunate that they have both been drawn in colour by the skilled hands of Norman and Nina de Garis Davies and published by the Egypt Exploration Society.

Besides mural paintings depicting scenes of family life and the fauna and flora of the Nile Valley, others have been found which represent the flowers and floral garlands that were employed to decorate the walls of rooms on festal occasions. In Old and Middle Kingdom tombs, above the scenes painted on the walls, there often appears a frieze representing papyrus heads tied together near the top. But with the Eighteenth Dynasty new forms of friezes come into fashion which were slightly conventionalised copies from nature of flowers that were used to decorate the tops of the walls. The two commonest types of these friezes were : (1) Lotus flowers alternating with lotus buds, and (2) lotus flowers alternating with bunches of blue grapes. These were drawn either standing erect or hanging down. The first type gave rise to those beautiful " lily-and-bud " friezes which adorn most Greek temples ; the second type is the original from which the " egg-and-tongue " ornament was evolved. Tiles of polychrome faience were occasionally employed in the palaces for wall decoration ; a few have been found at El Amarna of Ikhnaton's date, while others from Thebes and Tell el Yahudieh are of the time of Rameses III (P. 187).

The wall-spaces of the temples of the New Kingdom, like those of earlier periods, were decorated with scenes either painted on a thin coating of plaster, or sculptured in low relief, or in relief en creux, and then painted. In some of the mortuary chapels of the Nobles at Thebes, the walls were lined with mud, then coated with plaster and painted. Below the friezes were scenes illustrating the daily life of the people as well as the most important historical events of the time. In the unfinished chambers of the tombs of the Pharaohs Horemheb and Seti I in the Bibân el Muluk we can trace the various stages of the work from the setting out of the walls to the sculptor chiselling in relief the designs already drawn in black by an assistant draughtsman and corrected in red paint by the master-designer.

At Karnak and Der el Bahari there are many splendid specimens of sculpture in relief (Pp. 158 and 159) which date from the first half of the Eighteenth Dynasty ; they are instructive as showing that the traditions of the Middle Kingdom schools of art were still carried on by the designers of the New Kingdom. On comparing them with the reliefs of the Amenemhets and Senusrets the differences appear to be so slight that we might almost believe them to be contemporary. Naturally, many of the subjects treated are different from those found on the earlier monuments; for Egypt at this time was beginning to extend her frontiers, and foreign peoples with their art-products were coming into the country and were depicted in the scenes. Later in the Eighteenth Dynasty, under Amenhotep III, the sculpture in relief becomes even more delicate than in the days of Hatshepsut, and there is often extraordinary charm in the way the artist carries out his portraits of individuals. This is especially noticeable in the tombs of Khaemhet and Ramose at Thebes (P. 168). The latter tomb, dated in the reign of Amenhotep IV (before that monarch assumed the name of Ikhnaton and removed his capital to El Amarna), is of great importance in the history of Egyptian art, because in it we see scenes carried out according to the traditional canons of art, side by side with others in a style that at first sight appears to be new. This " new " style is supposed to have arisen under the direct influence of Ikhnaton himself, but a careful study of the paintings in the tombs at Thebes shows that some of its special features appear in the art of the period which immediately preceded him. As early as the reign of Thutmosis III the artists were beginning to break away from traditional designs in minor parts of their pictures, and we remark very accurate observation and exact drawing. In the tomb of Rekhmare, among the attendant women at a banquet, one is drawn on the half-turn precisely as a draughtsman of to-day would draw her. The banqueting scenes of this and subsequent reigns are treated far more realistically than in earlier periods ; the dancing girls and musicians are generally figured in the most charming postures, and are often full-faced instead of in profile (P. 160). On the body of the chariot of Thutmosis IV (P. 161), many of the foreigners are also represented in this way. In the hunting scenes of the period of Amenhotep II and Thutmosis IV, the wild animals are depicted, not with all four feet upon the ground as was usual earlier in the dynasty, but bounding along at full gallop. In the tomb of Kenamon there was a wonderful scene of wild animals in the desert which has unhappily suffered greatly at the hands of time. But enough remains of it to show that it was executed by an artist of the highest skill ; his realistic rendering of an ibex brought to bay by a hound is only equalled by the lions of the famous casket of Tutankhamen. Of all the painted tombs at Thebes— and there are hundreds of them—this one of Kenamon, an officer who served under Amenhotep II, is the finest. Norman de Garis Davies has copied this monument in its entirety; his verdict is that the designer employed in its decoration must have been " the best one of his day if not of his era."

When we examine the sculptured scenes in the tombs or on other monuments at El Amarna, we find the same naturalistic treatment, but an execution far inferior to the bas-reliefs of Amenhotep III's reign at Thebes. The subjects now chosen are nearly all connected with the Pharaoh and his new city; there are none of those beautiful hunting and fowling scenes (P. 160) which are so attractive in the tombs of earlier times. Ikhnaton was far too effeminate to indulge in the pleasures of the chase ; he preferred to drive around his city in the royal chariot with his wife and small children, and this theme is very successfully treated by the Court artists. He also appears adoring the Aten —the sun's disc (P. 164)—in the courtyard of the temple, or taking a meal with his Consort and daughters, or playing with his children (P. 165), or distributing gifts from the balcony of his palace. The designer had necessarily to abandon all the old " stock designs," for none of them was allowed to appear at El Amarna. The artists were thus able to adopt a freer and more sketchy style unhampered by the earlier canons of design. Much of this El Amarna drawing is of course pleasing, but the physical peculiarities of the king become so absurdly emphasised, distorted, and exaggerated, that Ikhnaton himself ultimately appears as the ugliest and most repulsive-looking person in Egyptian history (Pp. 164 and 173). Far finer in every way are the sculptured reliefs *en creux* of the tomb of the General Horemheb, which are now in the Leyden Museum (P. 166). These are from Memphis and date from Ikhnaton's period ; they give us a glimpse, and a glimpse only, at the designer's art that was then prevalent in that great city. Here, in the amazing portraits of foreigners, we see the Egyptian artist at his very best.

When Ikhnaton died and his successor returned to Thebes many of the draughtsmen and sculptors went back to the orthodox canons ; the reliefs in the temple at Luxor illustrating the triumphal return of Tutankhamen to Thebes are executed in this style, so also are the greater number of the scenes in Seti I's temple at Abydos (P. 168). But nothing can show more clearly this return to the old traditions of Thebes than to compare the sculptured scenes from the General Horemheb's Memphite tomb with those that are painted in his tomb at Thebes after he had seized the throne of Egypt (P. 166). The earlier scenes are in the freest style, the latter in the most conventional. It has been noticed, however, that in a few of the painted tombs at Thebes which date from the Ramesside period there is displayed a much greater freedom in the treatment of the subjects depicted. The tombs of Apy and Weserhet are the most important for the history of art under the Ramesside kings. They have both been published by Norman de Garis Davies in a volume of the Tytus Memorial Series issued by the Metropolitan Museum of Art. " The tomb of Apy " says Davies,[1] " belongs to a transition stage where the old and the new are combining in ever-varying proportions. There is no longer a fixed standard ; each artist with any power is an experiment to himself ; and, if the draughtsman and colourist of Apy's tomb has special idiosyncrasies, it is no doubt accounted for by the fact that Apy himself was a sculptor and may have been himself the executant. There is crowded into this little chamber much of the typical subject-matter of an Eighteenth Dynasty tomb ; but the form is quite changed and is one that, deadened and stereotyped, was to constitute the style of succeeding dynasties of Egyptian history." A typical painted interior of an official's tomb of the Nineteenth Dynasty is given in P. 167. On the lower part of the end wall is a scene showing the deceased man playing a game of draughts with his

---

[1] " Bulletin of the Metropolitan Museum of Art," New York, July, 1920, Part ii, p.27.

wife while their daughter looks on at the game. In place of the beautiful decorative designs that are seen in the tombs of the Eighteenth Dynasty, here are only figures of gods and men and large hieroglyphic inscriptions.

In no direction was the Egyptian's artistic faculty exercised with more consummate skill than in his sculpture in the round. To the period of the New Kingdom belongs a number of portraits of great merit, both in conception and in material execution. The earlier examples of the statuary of the Seventeenth Dynasty do not differ much in style from those of the end of the Middle Kingdom. A very charming portrait of a queen of this time is the little statuette of Tetisheri in the British Museum (P. 171). Slightly later in date is the electrum statuette of a boy, and the splendid gold statuette of the god Amon (P. 171), modelled in the likeness of Thutmosis III ; both these masterpieces of the metalworker's art are in the Metropolitan Museum of Art, New York. The portrait of Thutmosis III (P. 172) in fine grained basalt is another example of the same period ; here the sculptor has concentrated all his art upon the head of the great Pharaoh, and we see the monarch as he was in life. The statuette of his mother, the Queen Isis (P. 173), now in Cairo, represents her in formal attitude as a woman of middle life, seated on a chair; here the figure is conventional, but the face is obviously a true portrait. The group of a Mayor of Thebes seated with his wife and with their daughter standing between them (P. 174), is typical of the art of the middle of the Eighteenth Dynasty ; it should be observed here how the affectionate wife has her right arm around her husband's waist, his left arm round hers. Slightly later in date is the statue of the Scribe Amenhotep, son of Hapu (P. 175), who served under Amenhotep III, and in after-times was famous for his wisdom ; he is represented seated upon the ground and with slightly bent head is intent upon writing on the papyrus roll which is spread out upon his lap. It is interesting to compare this statue from Thebes, which is clearly the work of a Theban sculptor, with that of another seated Scribe—the Horemheb in the Metropolitan Museum of Art (P. 176), which is almost certainly from a Memphite artist's studio, and of Ikhnaton's date. This Horemheb is the Scribe and General who later in life succeeded King Ay on the throne of Egypt (see P. 34). Both sculptors adopted the realistic method, but how very differently they treat their subjects!

In one of the El Amarna tombs there is a relief that represents a sculptor's studio in full activity (N. de G. Davies, El Amarna, vol. III, Pl. XVIII) ; it was perhaps actually in this very workshop that the wonderful series of portrait heads modelled in plaster (P. 177) or sculptured in stone (P. 178) were executed. In the whole range of Egyptian art the examples from El Amarna are unsurpassed, and no Greek sculptor ever betrayed a finer feeling for purity of line. The sculptor's object here was a perfect likeness, and his rendering of life-like character in these portraits is astonishing. The plaster head of the Old Lady ranks among the masterpieces of the world, and is only equalled by the famous obsidian head of a Twelfth Dynasty monarch now in the possession of Mr. Gulbenkian (P. 129). The El Amarna sculptor, however, could work in more difficult material than plaster ; he was equally at home with crystalline sandstone, limestone and yellow jasper, and that the size of the statuette or statue was of as little concern as the material we see from the colossal figure of Ikhnaton from Karnak (P. 173). Colossal statues were a feature of this and the succeeding periods of Egyptian history. Two of Amenhotep III are still erect upon the Plain of Thebes, and many of Rameses II remain in the Temple at Luxor (P. 154).

Although the tomb of Tutankhamen has yielded a great number of beautiful pieces of furniture and other objects of daily use which are noticed in Doctor Howard Carter's chapter, a few specimens may be mentioned here which date from the periods immediately preceding and succeeding Tutankhamen's reign. The "Empire" chair of Amenhotep III's eldest daughter Satamen (P. 182) is a veritable triumph of the furniture-maker's craft ; so also is the exquisite Jewel Casket of Amenhotep III with its brilliant decoration in blue glazed faience and gold (P. 183). The toilet box and the perfume ladles (Pp. 180 and 181) show how the craftsman delighted to lavish upon objects of daily use all his inventive imagination. These objects are of fine-grained wood ; are purely Egyptian in origin and style, and are only known from the period of the New Kingdom.

JEWELLERY. Although the jewellery of the New Kingdom is inferior in technical skill to that of the Amenemhets and Senusrets of the Twelfth Dynasty, there is much to interest the jeweller among the surviving examples of his art. The technical processes are the same as in earlier periods, but they are not carried out with the same marvellous degree of accuracy. Furthermore, in the jewellery of the Middle Kingdom, real stones are invariably employed for inlay work, but in most of the examples of the New Kingdom the inlays are coloured glass imitating the semi-precious stones— turquoise, lapis lazuli, carnelian and red jasper. The most important jewels of the early days of the Eighteenth Dynasty are those of Ahmose I and of his Consort, Queen Ahhotep. These were discovered by Mariette at Thebes, and some now adorn the Jewel Room of the Cairo Museum, and others are in the Louvre. The armlets with amulet-boxes and gold sphinxes (P. 185) are noteworthy, for in design they are new. The dagger of Ahmose I, however, is the most interesting object of Mariette's " find." Its blade is of bronze with a central rib of gold, and on the gold is engraved a scene depicting a lion in " flying gallop " after a bull. Not so well known is a dagger bearing the name of a Hyksos king (P. 184). This foreign sovereign was probably a contemporary of Ahmose I, and on the gold hilt of his dagger is embossed a design showing a huntsman spearing a lion that is pursuing an antelope. The treatment of the lion leaping into the air is thought to be new to Egyptian art, and it has been suggested that this motive may have been an introduction from Minoan Crete.

Towards the middle of the Eighteenth Dynasty, under Thutmosis IV, new forms of necklaces appear, which under Amenhotep III and his immediate successors become very common; they last on in fashion till the reign of Rameses II or perhaps a little later. These necklaces consist of pendants in the form of flowers, leaves, and fruits, and it is now known that they were copied from the real floral garlands that were used at festivals and for adorning the bodies of the dead The flowers and fruits are typically Egyptian—lotuses, cornflowers, poppies, daisies, palm leaves, dates, mandrake fruits and pomegranates; all were grown in Egyptian gardens, and may be seen figured in the mural paintings of the tombs. These kinds of pendants are but rarely found modelled in gold, but one superb necklace of this type was brought to light at Enkomi in Cyprus, and is now in the British Museum. Some of its pendants have divisions on them that appear to have been filled with a vitreous paste—blue, white, and red. But if few examples in gold have been found in Egypt, imitations of them in polychrome faience, as well as the pottery moulds for making them, have been collected in thousands from the palaces, tombs and factories at Thebes, El Amarna, and Kantîr.

Of the jewellery of the later period there are many specimens to be seen in our museums. A gold and lapis lazuli bracelet bearing the cartouche of Rameses II is carried out with a perfect understanding of the goldsmith's art (P. 186). The ceremonial wig-ornaments of Seti II (P. 188) are modelled in the forms of seven poppy seed-vessels; the design is heavy and the workmanship coarse. Works of greater beauty are a necklace in gold filigree beads and pendants, a silver bracelet, and a gold chalice, all of which date from the reign of Queen Tausret (Pp. 186 and 188).

Of metal-work other than statuary and personal jewellery which can be dated to the

Fig. 6. Bronze bowl found at Thebes.

37

New Kingdom not much has survived. In the Louvre are gold bowls of shallow form of the reign of Thutmosis III; these are embossed in the centre with figures of swimming fish encircled by a border of papyrus reeds linked together by their stalks in a continuous pattern round the bowl. Of the same period are two copper-gilt bowls with a finely modelled cow standing erect in the middle of each. But the masterpiece of metal-worker's art is a beautifully chased bronze bowl belonging to the time of Ikhnaton that was found at Thebes, and is now in the Cairo Museum. The central medallion is engraved with a scene of a papyrus marsh in which there are bulls, cows, and a calf; one of the bulls is being attacked by a lion Among the reeds are birds and nests, the eggs in the latter are being robbed by ichneumons that have climbed the stems of the reeds. The frieze or narrow band running round the bowl is engraved with another marsh scene and in it are figured canoes paddled by boys—birds, fish, and a bull. The border is decorated with small engraved rosettes (P. 37, fig. 1).

CERAMICS AND GLASS. The history of these arts during the New Kingdom is one long record of success. In certain technical and artistic qualities, the wares of this time have never been surpassed. In the Leyden Museum there is a vase dating from the period immediately preceding the Seventeenth Dynasty which is glazed with blue of two shades of exquisite quality; this vase is identical in technique with some of the wares of Amenhotep II, Thutmosis IV and later kings. Faience bowls of the loveliest blues with ornamentation in manganese have been found in Seventeenth Dynasty tombs at Thebes, and similar bowls can be dated to the reigns of Hatshepsut, Thutmosis III, Amenhotep II and Thutmosis IV. The motifs of their decoration are lotus flowers and leaves, fish in pools, geometrical designs and sometimes human figures and animals. The scope of the potter's palette was now extended by several new colours, a yellow often deepening into orange, a white of extraordinary purity, an opaque red like that which, two and a half millenniums later, is found in the Kutayia and so-called "Rhodian" wares of Asia Minor. Black glaze was also employed, as well as some lovely greens and violets. Many objects of faience with splendid coloration have been found in the palaces at Thebes and El Amarna. Among them are a number of imitation gold and other metal finger-rings inlaid with imitation gems. The gold is imitated by a brilliant yellow glaze; silver by white; and the gems are represented by glazes closely approximating lapis lazuli, turquoise and red jasper in colour. Polychrome tiles (P. 187), which were employed for the decoration of the walls of palaces at Thebes, El Amarna, Tell el Yahudiyeh and Kantîr, demonstrate the extraordinary proficiency of the ceramic art of the New Kingdom. Henry Wallis, writing of the tiles from the palace of Rameses III at Tell el Yahudiyeh, remarks that all the resources of art were employed on them. "We find therein bas-relief, inlaying and a palette of the widest range. Nothing can be imagined in ceramic art more masterly than the modelling of the human figures and animal forms. The types of the different nationalities represented in the tiles are seized with an accuracy that may be termed scientific ; their costumes display a wealth of details worked out in schemes of colour so resplendent and harmonious as to delight all artists." Since Wallis wrote, another series of wall-tiles, in better preservation than those he saw, has been discovered in the ruins of the palace of Rameses III at Medinet Habu, and is now in the Cairo Museum. Manipulative dexterity of the first order is also shown in the glass cups and vases of the reigns of Thutmosis III (P. 189), Amenhotep II, Thutmosis IV, Amenhotep III and Ikhnaton, as well as in the series of blue glazed faience chalices (Pp. 189 and 190) from Tuneh which are assigned to the Twentieth and Twenty-second Dynasties. These chalices are modelled in the shape of half-opened lotus flowers with a stalk which expands and flattens out to form the foot.

TEXTILES. There is little doubt that many of the beautiful ceiling patterns in the tombs of the Nobles at Thebes really represent tapestry-woven, as well as appliqué leather, hangings ; others are obviously derived from the mat-worker's craft. In the patterns is displayed a great variety of design, and some of the most beautiful are to be seen in the tombs of Imisibe and Nespenefrhor at Thebes ; the former dates from the reign of Rameses IX, the latter from the reign of the Priest-king Herihor. Of the Twenty-first Dynasty is the magnificent Funeral Tent of Queen Isitemkheb in leather appliqué which adorns the Central Hall of the Cairo Museum.

Less than forty years ago the only textiles known from Dynastic times in Egypt were plain white linens of texture varying from the finest cambric to the coarsest canvas. But at the beginning of the present century a wholly new light was thrown on the history of the art of weaving by the discovery of some tapestry-woven fragments in the tombs of Amenhotep II and Thutmosis IV. One of these, a piece of a corselet of Amenhotep II, is illustrated in colour (P. 169). The cloth was, of course, originally white, the ornamentation being tapestry-woven in coloured linen threads ; the dyes used were blue, red, green, yellow, and brown outlined in black. Another fragment bears the name of Thutmosis III, and this important discovery carries back the history of tapestry-weaving some thousand years earlier than it had before been known. But here in these pieces of the New Kingdom we see the art at its best, and no finer tapestry-weaving is known from any period. There is nothing in the designs to suggest that they were foreign importations, and these small relics show how little is really known about the history of some of the crafts of the people who dwelt on the banks of the Nile.

P. E. NEWBERRY

THE REIGN OF TUTANKHAMEN

THERE can be little doubt that Tutankhamen belonged to a period when Egyptian art had reached a very high standard of excellence, but because of the discovery of his tomb, and because we have a complete series of the arts and crafts of his reign, we must not consequently be carried away with the idea that the arts of his age have necessarily greater merit than those of any other Egyptian period. What we really owe to the extent of the discovery is a more complete insight into the arts and crafts of his brief period in the Imperial Age of Egypt.

Fundamentally the same in all essentials common to Egyptian art, the art of the New Empire was more Upper than Lower Egyptian in character. The artist of Upper Egypt, according to his nature and his environment, loved to attenuate details and soften his modelling. The Lower Egyptian, preferred sturdy, robust types like himself, with salient muscles and broad shoulders. But, being still under the trammels of certain conventions, Upper Egyptian art achieved liberty only by the accident of individual inspiration.

The art of Tutankhamen's reign is characterized by extraordinary technical skill, and a suspicion of exotic influence which made it less motionless. As a consequence of the foundation of the Empire by Thothmes III, this new feature in Egyptian art begins to show itself during the second half of the Eighteenth Dynasty, notably at the time of Thothmes IV, and even more forcibly in the reign of Amenhetep III. By being transferred to El-Amarna, and by the elimination of a multitude of gods resulting from the new heresy, Upper Egyptian art was released from those impediments which checked freer movement; it also became more intimate. Subsequently this art, being liberated from the personal idiosyncrasies of the religious deportee, Akhenaten, who dreamt his life away at El-Amarna, reaches its zenith in this reign.

The capital of Akhenaten was abandoned, the Court was removed back to Thebes, the State religion reverted to the old Amen worship; yet the artist was freer to show his powers of invention, although commanded to make additions and restorations to the Theban temples, to fashion stutues of the Theban gods, and to reproduce stereotyped ceremonial scenes, such as the king in communion with the gods, and the celebration of festivals. This feeling of expression on the part of the artist is exhibited by the sculptured reliefs of Tutankhamen in the temple of Luxor, depicting the voyage of the god Amen and his divine companions to the celebration of the festival of the " Southern Temple." On that occasion the sacred boats of the gods were brought from Karnak to Luxor, borne into the Temple, and returned to Karnak at the end of the festival. In these reliefs the procession is depicted in a more realistic manner in all its interesting details.

Fig. 5.   Relief of the Reign of Tutankhamen at Luxor.
From a pencil drawing by Howard Carter

An intimate tendency in this art becomes apparent in pictures like that on the back of Tutankhamen's throne (P. 192)—a simple, homely composition. Instead of an austere Pharaoh on a throne, we have the man himself seated in unconventional attitude upon a cushioned chair, his arm thrown carelessly across its back.   Before him stands the girlish figure of the queen, putting, apparently, the last touches to his toilet : in one hand she holds a small jar of scent or ointment, and with the other she gently anoints his shoulder or adds a touch of perfume to his collar.   This feeling is again found on the gold covering of a miniature shrine, where there is a series of small panels, in low relief, depicting, in naïve fashion, episodes in the daily life of the king and queen (P. 193).   One in particular has almost a humorous element. The queen, accompanying the king on a shooting expedition, is represented crouching at his feet.   With one hand she offers him an arrow, with the other she points out a fat duck which she fears may escape his notice.   On a box, veneered with ivory, is another domestic scene, carved in delicate low relief like a Greek coin (P. 194).   The royal couple are represented in a pavilion bedecked with festoons of flowers, and the vine.   The king, leaning slightly on his walking-staff, accepts bouquets from his charming consort ; while, in a frieze below, the court maidens gather flowers and the fruit of the mandrake for their charges.   In all these scenes the dominant note is one of amiable relationship, the unselfconscious friendliness that marks the " El Amarna-Tutankhamen " style.   This intimacy is also noticeable in the plastic art of the period, for instance, in the little gold figure of the boy king upon a ceremonial stick, probably borne by a groom-in-waiting on State occasions.   The statuette portrays a graceful figure of sedate but youthful bearing, the gesture of the hands is of youthful simplicity, in fact, the boy being more apparent than the king (P. 195).

The exotic feature in this art arrests attention in scenes such as are found on a painted casket (Pp. 196-7)—one of the greatest treasures of the period. Its outer face is completely covered with gesso ; upon this prepared surface there are a series of brilliantly coloured designs—hunting scenes upon the curved panels of the lid, battle scenes upon the sides, and upon the ends representations of the king in lion form, trampling Egypt's enemies under his feet. The motives of these paintings are Egyptian and the treatment Egyptian, and yet they leave an impression on the mind of something strangely non-Egyptian. They remind one of the finest Persian miniatures, and there is a curious floating impression of Benozzo Gozzoli, of the fifteenth-century Florentine School, due, it may be, to the tufts of flowers which fill the vacant spaces. In the war scenes, Tutankhamen, for the sake of effect no longer a slender youth, is shooting down his enemies by hundreds from his chariot ; panic is before him, the dead at his feet. Such pictures of Egyptian kings are, of course, traditional. They are probably, in the case of our young monarch, merely the customary homage of the court painter. Take, for instance, the hunting-scenes. They are full of the sense of speed and movement. The king in his chariot, drawn by steeds gorgeous in their trappings, is seen thundering down the wady-bed pursuing desert fauna. Before him flee antelope and ostrich, wild-ass and hyena—all the denizens of the desert, including lions and lionesses. Seen between the figures of the animals and the feet of his followers are gay tufts of desert flora forming the scrub of the wady. These pictures, like the battle-scenes, are traditional. They are idealized scenes, wherein the spirit of the chase has been vividly captured and interpreted. The artist of this period must have had the sense of space and line, and appreciation of detail. The agonized beasts are rendered with utmost realism. There are moments—in the group of hunted lions, for example—when the painter reaches almost tragic power. One of the lions —the king beast—stricken to the heart, having sprung into the air in the final spasm of death, is seen falling headlong to the ground. Another clutches with his paw at a shaft which has entered his open mouth, and hangs broken in his jaws ; meanwhile the half-grown cub is slinking away with tail between its legs, whilst wounded comrades lie in tortured postures of pathetic suffering.

The variety of attitude found in the Egyptian paintings and reliefs is lacking in the statues. A peculiarity of Egyptian plastic art, throughout its long history, is that all figures, standing or sitting, walking or motionless, confront the spectator ; and it would seem that deviation from the law of frontal presentment—or as it has been called, " The Law of Frontality "—was forbidden. The incongruities such as are found in their reliefs and paintings —the absence of any kind of foreshortening, of the picture built up of undiminished parts, of complex objects shown mentally reconstructed—are comprehensible, since the laws of perspective that render accurately visual impression were then undiscovered ; but why the plastic arts in Egypt should have been governed by an almost parallel convention is, to us, more difficult to understand. However, this frontal presentment |is less conspicuous in some of the statuettes of this reign, especially in the gracious little figures of the tutelary goddesses discovered guarding the canopic chest in Tutankhamen's tomb (P. 200). One guarded the chest on each side, but whereas the figures at the front and back kept their gaze firmly fixed upon their charge, an additional note of realism was imparted by the other two, for their heads were turned sideways, looking over their shoulders, as though to watch against surprise. In a less degree, this slight turn of the head is found on a walking-stick (P. 195), on the curved handle of which are the figures of a pair of bound captives, the one an African, the other an Asiatic, their faces carved in ebony and ivory respectively. The head of the Asiatic, of Semitic character, is an almost painfully realistic piece of work ; but the African, equally fine, turns his head upward in bitter distress.

Another character peculiar to Egyptian statuary is that its figures have a stolidity whether represented moving or motionless. This is a great deal due to that unconscious frontal presentment, and to the fact that Egyptian statues almost invariably have the full weight of the body on both soles of the feet. This convention is but a natural result of an art keeping so strictly within the limitations of its media, and unconscious of visual impression. Among the works of Tutankhamen's reign, however, monotony of this kind is diversified in the figure of " The King Harpooning " (P. 198). This is almost Hellenistic in style, the movement, and the manner in which the weight of the body is thrown on to the left foot, are realistically suggested. Equally skilful, but more conventional, are " The King upon a Leopard " (P. 199) and the life-size black wooden statues that once stood on either side of the doorway of the burial chamber in the tomb (P. 202). But these have a placidity and lightness peculiar to Tutankhamen work. Even among the numerous little austere statuettes, known as " Shawabti" (P. 201), manufactured and placed in the grave to act as servants for the deceased, a serene yet cheerful kind of portraiture can be found. But hardly any specimen surpasses the magnificent gold mask (P. 204) from the head of the king's mummy. Conventional as it may be, it is a true likeness of Tutankhamen at the age of his death. As Dr. Derry said : " Those who were privileged to see the actual face (of the mummy) when finally exposed can bear testimony to the ability and accuracy of the Eighteenth Dynasty artist, who had so faithfully represented the features, and left them for all time, in imperishable metal, a beautiful portrait of the young king."

The gold mask and the gold coffin that enclosed Tutankhamen's mummy testify that the artistic handicrafts had reached a high degree of perfection at this period of the New Empire. The Theban goldsmiths must have attained complete mastery of their craft to carry out such elaborate work within the short period (a few months) intervening between the death and the burial of the king. To realize fully the extent of their work carried out in so short a time we must take into consideration not only the preparation, beating, modelling and chasing of the gold, but the subordinate art of incrustation with coloured natural stones, glass and faience, with which both the coffin and the mask were embellished. Of this ancillary art of incrustation, the second coffin of Tutankhamen is a wonderful specimen : it is made of wood, overlaid with thin sheet-gold, and inlaid with polychrome glass. But in the work of those coffins, I might even add in the mask, there is nothing of the intimate or exotic details that attract attention in other works of the period. They are essentially Egyptian. They retain all the conventions of the art and the burial traditions of those ancient peoples. They are influenced by a traditional religious conception : from the moment death had taken place the deceased was regarded as Osiris, and it became a condition of primary importance that the deceased should be the image of that deity ; the face may remain a portrait, but the body and accessories must represent the form with attributes of the god. The world in general seldom appreciates what it does not understand, and there is much that is strange to us in these pieces. The difference one feels is this : whilst the art belonging to the reign of Tutankhamen retains the ancient traditions, it has in addition an intimate charm and sense of movement—one is almost tempted to say a modern charm—characteristic of itself (Pp. 191 and 203).

The jewellers' work is far more flamboyant than any hitherto found. Their crafts included that of the lapidary, of the glass-cutter, inlaying, chasing, repoussé-work, embossing, twisted gold wire filigree work, and granulated gold-work. This last (Pp. 204-6) is a prominent feature in their jewellery, and comprises a decoration of minute spherical grains of gold in all probability fused or sweated to the curved or flat gold surfaces of the objects treated. Many of their ornaments were worked *a jour*, upon which various semi-precious stones and polychrome glass were inlaid, either in high or low relief, or quite flat in " cloisonné " fashion. It must, however, be understood that the term " cloisonné," as applied to Egyptian jewellery, may be misleading. It really means that stones or their glass and faience substitutes were cemented into the metal cells or " cloisons," and that the incrustation was not enamel as in the case of true " cloisonné " work. Enamel was unknown to the ancient Egyptians. The metals employed in their jewellery were gold, electrum, silver, and in a less degree copper and bronze ; the natural stones were amethyst, turquoise, lapis lazuli, calcite, carnelian, chalcedony, green felspar, semi-translucent and translucent quartz often backed with pigment

44

for brilliance and imitative effects, serpentine, and several hard ornamental stones not yet identified. Besides these they employed composite materials such as faience (glazed pottery), hard vitreous pastes, semi-transparent and opaque coloured glasses, used in the place of some one or other of the above mentioned stones. Perhaps the most remarkable material sometimes used in the composition of their jewellery was a dark coloured resin. Another peculiarity of the period was a means employed to give to some gold a scarlet tint. This scarlet-tinted gold, when overlaid with a bright yellow gold ornamentation, imparted a peculiarly brilliant but somewhat barbaric effect.

Strangely novel, yet typical of the age, are the skilful works of the stone-carver. His ornate vessels wrought of semi-translucent alabaster evoke surprise mingled with curiosity and admiration. Their strange forms seem almost to belong to wonderland. The wishing-cup and the tricerion have a particular charm ; but the remarkable objects in this class of work are the perfume vases with their flanking ornamentation, the cosmetic-jar with a recumbent lion on its lid, and the quaintly heraldic vase in the shape of a lion standing upright in an aggressive attitude ; or the " centre-piece " in the form of a boat, with a little figure of a nude girl on the fore-deck, and a puny dwarf at the helm : one cannot but observe how beautifully and how accurately those female figures, as well as the ibex heads on the stem and stern, have been rendered by the court stone-carver who wrought that fascinating ornament (Pp. 207-210).

The excellence of the craft of the joiner is well exemplified by the examples of furniture discovered in the tomb (Pp. 211-217). The quality of these suggests a high state of civilization, proficiency, ingenuity, and a sound sense of design. Among the beautifully carved bedsteads and chairs, stools and chests, and the curious animal-sided couches, glistening with gold and inlay, the distinctive specimens that mark the artistic trend of that moment are : the throne ; a cedar-wood chair, elaborately and delicately carved ; a little chair, with decorative panels of ebony, ivory and gold, and a red-wood trellis-work stool inlaid with ivory and ebony, both too small for other than a child's use ; a casket, standing upon four slim legs, which has all the aspects of what it pleases us to call modern workmanship ; and a large chest, made of a delightful combination of ebony, ivory and red-wood, having sliding poles underneath by which to carry it. But the marquetery decoration with variegated barks comes to us somewhat as a surprise. This artistic handiwork of the joiner and the bowyer is particularly observable on the king's bow-case and bows, and even upon some of the walking-sticks. It comprises a very fine marquetery veneer of different coloured barks, applied thin strips of tinted leather, and gold foil, with, in some instances, blue and green iridescent beetles' wings. The reign of Tutankhamen, like the different ages of ancient Egypt, is distinguished by certain individuality of taste, and particularly so by this unique kind of bark and beetle-wing veneer that affords such harmonious colour. It not only appeals to the æsthetic sense, but, to us, it creates an admiration of the patient and skilful workmanship on the part of those ancient Egyptian craftsmen. It implies, too, the existence of keen and efficient implements. Another form of decoration was a marquetry inlay of minute pieces of ivory and ebony. A great number of small shapen pieces were arranged to form diamond, criss-cross, and herring-bone patterns, within panels formed by a veneer of broad strips of ivory. As is usual in all such cabinet-makers' art, the basic wood was of poorer quality ; and over this inferior body the more valuable materials forming the marquetry inlay and veneer were laid by means of a glue adhesive. Some 45,000 pieces of inlay have been employed in the ornamentation of a single casket.

For examples of simple ivory carving, I must refer the reader to a small jewel box of exquisite proportions, and a head-rest which is perhaps the finest piece of Egyptian New Empire symbolical art hitherto discovered. The theme of its design seems to be an impression of the official religion, and its subject founded upon one of the early conceptions of the cosmos, when all things fell into their places. The myth represented conceives Geb and Nut, the Earth god and the Sky goddess, as husband and wife, separated by their father Shu, the god of Atmosphere. The observer cannot but be sensible of the serenity of this little monument, inspired, it would seem, by a kindly feeling : the king when at rest would lay his head in heaven and, maybe, become a star in the firmament (P. 218).

The Egyptians were the inventors of glazes and glass. These manufactures are well represented in the Tutankhamen collection by two very fine head-rests—one of turquoise blue glass, the other a gorgeous piece of work in rich lapis lazuli blue glazed pottery (P. 219)—not to mention numerous small vessels of the same material that were found among the kings' funerary equipment.

Unfortunately, all textile fabrics in the tomb had suffered deterioration set up by damps from infrequent saturations that had occurred during the long past. But, although they have fallen into decay, their remains are sufficient to show that the textile arts had reached a high standard of excellence. Linen garments and gloves richly ornamented with tapestry-woven decoration, and in some cases needlework, were the court fashion at this period (P. 220).

Freer movement, the intimate and the exotic elements in this art were little more than a dream. One by one they disappeared. There was no sudden extinction. They faded away. The god Amen seems to have diffused austerity as a hayfield diffuses scent, not only over the temple and tomb, but over the artistic temperament of the people. Painting and sculpture were, within their conventions, never more modern in spirit than during the brief reign of Tutankhamen.

HOWARD CARTER

THE SAÏTE, PTOLEMAIC AND ROMAN PERIODS

THE art of Egypt during its later period was in many ways only a repetition or an imitation of the work of earlier ages. Its close adherence to tradition and its intense conservatism were such that it is not easy for those who have not made a special study of the subject to distinguish a statue or other work of art of the Twenty-sixth Dynasty from similar examples of earlier date. Indeed, the works of the earliest and finest periods were often deliberately copied in later times. The great majority of the works of this later period are lacking in life and individuality, and merely vary in the amount of technical skill with which they imitate their models. But, from time to time, we find examples of observation and expression such as hardly appear at first sight to be at all characteristic of Egyptian art. It is true that we find remarkable instances of realistic portraiture from the early dynasties, such as the well-known Sheikh-el-Beled ; and also that the art of Akh-en-aten, contemporary with that of Minoan Crete, often shows a tendency to naturalistic forms, not only in decorative work, but also in the human figure, amounting almost to caricature. But there is something new and different in the examples that occur about the time of the Twenty-sixth Dynasty. It is difficult to trace any foreign influence in these, for we know of no other national art from which they could be derived. The art of Greece, which influenced Egypt under the Thirtieth Dynasty and later, was not yet sufficiently advanced to exert such influence, and indeed was borrowing from Egypt many elements which it was later to combine and develop in its own way. Several examples of this realistic tendency, standing out conspicuously among the mass of conventional and imitative work, will come before us in their due place.

The temples and other buildings of the Saïte Period are for the most part very imperfectly preserved ; but both in plan and in decoration they appear to have followed very closely the traditions of earlier ages, and to have handed them on to the architects of the Ptolemaic and Roman Periods, who, like their earlier predecessors, had greater resources at their disposal, and so were enabled to rival the colossal structures of the second Theban age. The best preserved temple of the Saïte Period is that of Horus at Edfu (P. 222), which, however, conforms pretty closely to the general plan and effect of temples of the Ramesside age, though with some differences of detail. An example of the temples of Ptolemaic times may be seen in Denderah (Pp. 222, 224), with its four-sided Hathor capitals. Another is to be seen at Kom Ombo (P. 223). For work of the Roman Period a well-known example is the small pavilion of the time of Hadrian or Trajan at Philæ (P. 221), which, as Maspéro observes, " was to later centuries what Karnak had been to the earlier ages, the favoured spot where all the sovereigns had worked uninterruptedly, and consequently where the successive phases of the evolution of art may be most clearly observed." In these buildings, beside a general conformity to tradition, there is a certain variation in detail and a power of evolving new forms, or new combinations of old forms, which show that art has not entirely lost its creative power. There is, however, a tendency to over-loading of decoration and to a mingling of various architectural forms. But the colossal size of some of the temples makes them very impressive.

It is above all in sculpture that it is possible to recognize the originality of some artists amidst a general mass of uniformity. A typical example of such work in the Twenty-fifth Dynasty is the portrait head of Tirhaka (P. 226). The racial character of this head may be due to an intrusive Ethiopian strain. There is a certain coarseness and even brutality about the workmanship as well as about the character represented ; but the skill in working the hard and intractable material shows a strong artistic tradition. The same may be said of the portrait of Mentuemhat (P. 226, fig. 2), one of the most remarkable productions of later Egyptian sculpture. He was a ruler of Thebes toward the end of the Twenty-fifth Dynasty, and had evidently a very efficient and vigorous character. This is shown by the strongly marked features and deeply-cut wrinkles, and a curiously modern effect is given by the unusual wig and the realistically treated chin-beard. The small and narrow eyes, fleshy cheeks, massive jaw and heavy lips are evidently individual characteristics ; the portrait thus offers a contrast both to the majestic and idealizing conceptions of earlier times and to the great mass of conventional work. Another statue of the later years of the Twenty-fifth Dynasty is that of the Queen Amenartas (P. 225). This is of alabaster. The face, while it has a somewhat exaggerated and strained expression, is full of life ; but the whole figure, as in much Egyptian sculpture, is purely conventional, moulding the bodily forms as if through thick yet transparent drapery.

There is a remarkable portrait of an old man in the British Museum. It is in quartzite sandstone, and probably represents a Theban noble. In the official description it is called " one of the finest examples of the Theban school of portrait sculptors in the eighth-seventh century B.C., which produced portraits rivalling those of the Twelfth Dynasty in fidelity but distinguished from them by a greater delicacy." The refined modelling of the face and the carefully observed but not exaggerated wrinkles around the mouth and upper eyelids show an idealizing tendency in great contrast to the brutal realism of such a portrait as that of Mentuemhat (P. 227).

The Hathor Cow in Cairo, with the Scribe Psammetichus standing in front of it, offers a good opportunity for comparison with an earlier version of a

Fig. 6. Relief of Psammetichus I.
British Museum

similar subject, the famous Hathor Cow with Amenophis II from Deir-el-Bahari. This cow, in yellow sandstone, is a delicate and sensitive piece of work, carefully studied from the real animal ; but that of Psammetichus is a more or less mechanical repetition, though the technical skill with which the hard material, green basalt, is treated, the fineness of the finish and the correctness of the modelling show a high level of artistic tradition (Pp. 157 and 231).

Among portraits of the Twenty-sixth Dynasty one of the most remarkable is a relief in the British Museum representing the King Psammetichus I, on a slab of black basalt. The figure is merely conventional ; but the face, seen in profile, is evidently a realistic portrait, showing clearly the character of the wily adventurer and self-made man. Another relief, that of Za-Nefer in Alexandria (P. 228), shows notable originality in its figures, especially in the face of the old man playing a triangular harp. His features are modelled with great delicacy, showing but not exaggerating the traces of advanced age in his hooked nose and hollow cheek. And the other figures in the same relief are not merely mechanical repetitions of the same type, but show individuality not only in the faces but also in the arrangement of the drapery, which has an appearance more Greek than Egyptian. And, in the time of Psammetichus, with his " bronze men " from over the sea, the fashions of Ionia may not have been unknown to the Egyptian artists.

The green basalt head of an old man, now in Berlin, was broken from a statue, and found at Memphis (P. 229). It represents with unsparing realism every wrinkle and every delicately modelled play of surface in the hard and brilliantly polished stone. At first sight it reminds us of the portrait studies of Roman or even of Tuscan art. But the conventional pillar at the back is characteristically Egyptian ; and the statue must be of far earlier date than any similar approach to realism in Greek or Roman work. It merely adds a higher degree of exactness and delicacy to such portrait art as is occasionally found in the Saïte Period. As Sir F. Petrie points out, " the bony structure, the facial muscles, and the surface folds are all scrupulously observed. The artist's triumph is shown in the harmony and the living character he has infused into his laborious precision. Very rarely can a man rise superior to such a rigorous training."

Though this is the most remarkable portrait of its kind, others are known which are of a somewhat similar style and material. An example may be seen in a youthful clean-shaven head in Berlin which is smoother and more generalised in form, but shows a similar mastery in the treatment of hard material and power of expression (P. 230).

A very different kind of art is to be seen in the bronze statue of Takushet in Athens (P. 231). The forms of the body, visible in the usual Egyptian fashion through the clinging drapery, are plump and rounded, and the features of the face lack distinction. But the craftsmanship of the delicate ornamentation of all the dress is very noteworthy. It consists of a series of Egyptian mythological representations, rendered in fine line work by inlaid silver wire, so as to give a very rich effect. Small statues and statuettes in bronze, both of gods and men, are very common during this period, and are often of finer workmanship than contemporary work in stone.

During the period of Persian rule, not much artistic work seems to have been done in Egypt ; but under the Thirtieth Dynasty, the last age of Egyptian independence, there was some revival of sculpture and painting. Much of it, however, shows the influence of Greek art, which had now, in the fourth century B.C., attained to its highest perfection. It cannot be said that the mingling of Egyptian and Hellenic elements was always a happy one. Sometimes the character of the work remains mainly Egyptian, but with more preference for roundness of form and softness of effect. In other cases the work is mainly Greek, and only some details or peculiarities reveal an Egyptian origin. It is interesting to compare the portrait relief of Nectanebo, dated about 358 B.C. with the similar relief of Psammetichus. Both alike are carved in hollow relief in black basalt ; but while the figure of Psammetichus is almost flat within its outline, that of Nectanebo has a delicately modelled play of surface. But on the other hand the head of Nectanebo is of a more conventional type, and does not show the same remarkable individuality of character which may be seen in the features of Psammetichus. The development of Greek sculpture, from its early experiments to the full attainment of its perfection, lies in date between these two Egyptian portraits, and although the form of both is characteristically Egyptian, the earlier shows an uncouth vigour and the later an accomplished finish due probably to Greek influence (P. 232).

Many of the works we have been considering belong to the period which is more or less contemporary with the rise of Greek sculpture. There is, however, an early Ionic vase, coming from the home of those very mercenaries who were employed and favoured by Psammetichus and Amasis, which shows us how these Greeks thought of the Egyptians. It illustrates a story which is evidently of Greek and not Egyptian origin, and tells how a certain King Busiris, unknown to Egyptian records, was in the habit of sacrificing all strangers who arrived in Egypt. The Greek hero Heracles was thus captured and intended as a victim, but he broke his fetters and turned the tables on his

Fig. 7. Heracles slaying Busiris

captors, slaying Busiris and his guards. The scene, as depicted on the vase, is of the nature of caricature ; but it is an interesting study of various racial types, the massive and ruddy Greek, the two kinds of Egyptians with their yellow and black complexions, and the guard of negroes who hasten to the rescue. The king is distinguished by the uraeus snake above his forehead.

Among Egyptian products that show clear signs of Greek influence is a series of mummy-shaped sarcophagi in various materials. In some the face is carved, in others painted only. One, which probably belongs to the fourth century B.C., is carved in wood. The whole body and drapery, with the representation of wings folded about the lower limbs, is of Egyptian type. But the head might be, and perhaps is the work of a Greek artist, and shows the regular classical features that are usual in Greek work of this period. The hair, too, is simply and naturally arranged over the forehead, though the top of the head and the sides are covered by a richly decorated feather head-dress. The eyes have bronze sockets in which some vitreous filling is inserted. The whole was probably gilt, so that the graining of the wood, now too conspicuous, would be concealed (P. 233).

A monument of about 300 B.C., the beginning of the Ptolemaic Period, is the tomb of Pet-Osiris. Much of the decoration of this tomb is purely Egyptian, but there are also many coloured reliefs which show a strange blending of Egyptian subjects with Greek forms and technique. In the portion of the decoration of the pronaos completing that shown on P. 235 the central position is taken by a tomb-shrine of simple design. In front of it and beside it are grouped the members of the deceased's family, children in the middle, and groups of men and women on either side. These are treated with freedom from any Egyptian convention ; a group in particular, on the left of the scene, represents a woman in Greek drapery, leaning on a pillar, and a man beside her, leaning on her shoulder, in a manner which recalls Greek sculptures and reliefs. Other decorations from this tomb contain lists of offerings and hieroglyphic inscriptions which are purely Egyptian ; others again show scenes familiar in Egyptian art, such as mowing the harvest, but treated with a naturalism in detail and a freedom of drawing that are clearly due to Greek influence. It is a curious coincidence that some of these scenes recall the paintings in Etruscan tombs ; but the explanation is not, probably, to be sought in any direct relation between the two, but rather in the coincidence of a similar blend of a phase of Hellenistic art with that of a technically accomplished people with a different artistic tradition.

A porcelain head with a greeny-blue glaze, found at Naucratis and now in the British Museum, may probably be identified as a portrait of an early Ptolemaic queen, Arsinoe, the consort of Ptolemy II, whom she married in 279 B.C. It certainly has a striking resemblance to the head of Arsinoe on coins, in the projecting nose and chin, rounded at the end, the receding forehead, and rather prominent eyes. The style is Greek rather than Egyptian, but the material and technique are common in Egypt at various periods, especially in beads, scarabs and ushabti ; but a Greek portrait in this material is exceptional, and gives this head a place among works of sculpture rather than among decorative examples. Its size is quite small, only about $2\frac{1}{2}$ inches or 60 millimetres in height ; and the modelling, on this small scale, is delicate and refined (P. 246, fig. 3).

A fairly typical example of the monumental portraiture of the later Ptolemaic era may be seen in the portrait of Ptolemy Auletes (P. 234), father of the well-known Cleopatra. This is of basalt, in the British Museum, and shows technical skill and polish in working a hard material. The expression is somewhat exaggerated, and the forms are heavy and rounded ; but it appears as if the likeness was well caught. Reliefs of about the same period are to be seen at Kom Ombo and elsewhere. The one here reproduced shows the king amid a group of Egyptian gods (P. 235). The work is ornate and delicate in detail, but there is a roundness and plumpness in the forms both of body and faces, such as may be seen in other reliefs of the time. The over elaborate effect of a whole temple covered with such work may be realized from the views of the temple at Denderah (P. 224). A relief from Denderah shows Cleopatra herself. The form of the features, especially the hooked outline of the nose and full chin, are evidently personal characteristics which reappear on her coins. But the whole effect is very conventional, and the shape of the body is almost deformed in appearance, with one breast only represented and that in semi-globular profile. This and the comparative shapelessness of the limbs are found in other reliefs of about the same time. The rendering of hair and head-dress is elaborate, but differs from earlier Egyptian fashions (P. 236).

It is interesting to compare with these later Egyptian works showing the influence of Greek art an example in which a conception originally derived from Egypt is given a purely Greek form. This is the case with the god Sarapis, whose position in earlier Egyptian religion is somewhat obscure, but whose worship had a great vogue in the Hellenistic and Roman world. As a god of healing, also associated with the lower world, the type under which the Greek sculptor represented him was derived from that of Zeus or of Asclepius; but there is a certain sombreness and mystery about the expression which suggests the attitude of the Greeks to Egyptian deities. The small basket-like crown on the head is also borrowed from Egyptian custom. The origin of the type is doubtful; the first example is said to have been created by the sculptor Bryaxis, or brought by Ptolemy from Sinope or Antioch. But the worship of Sarapis spread over a large area of the civilised world, and only yielded in the fourth century in the struggle with Christianity. He was thought of as lord of the world of death, and his mildness joined with melancholy may be derived from this conception (P. 239).

A curious mingling of Greek and Egyptian work may sometimes be found in statuettes, such as that on P. 241 (figs. 4 and 5). At first sight, this may well be taken for a nude female figure of Greek style, but on closer observation, it is evident that the sculptor has followed the Egyptian custom of modelling the whole figure in a general kind of way, though the drapery only shows clearly between the legs and round the feet. But the modelling of the torso through the drapery shows the complete freedom of later Greek art.

In the Roman period imitations of earlier Egyptian work continue to be produced; the most remarkable among them are portraits. That of the priest Horus of Alexandria, for example, has a very refined and intellectual type of face, rendered with great delicacy; the drapery, which is somewhat summarily treated, is of Greek, not Egyptian fashion, a custom common in this period, and the pose is conventional, the left arm drawing the garment across the front of the torso (P. 238, fig. 1).

Perhaps the most remarkable of all these Romano-Egyptian portraits is that of Julius Cæsar (P. 237), of black basalt, in the Barracco collection in Rome. It shows the rigid and severe craftsmanship suitable to the material that was already seen in some heads of the Twenty-seventh Dynasty; but here there is a new element in the keenly intellectual type and the strength of genius. If Egyptian in technique, the head shows also the realistic portraiture of republican Rome. The closely cropped hair and beard, the deep and clearly incised wrinkles on brow and forehead, the delicately modelled lips, all make this a masterpiece of portraiture, and give us the most vivid impression of the great conqueror and organiser. Yet even such a convention as the supporting pillar at the back of the head is retained. In contrast to this magnificent head, we may take a statuette in the British

Museum (P. 240, fig. 2), an old man. The drapery is Greek in form, and shows the attitude, common at this time, of the fold drawn across the body by the left hand; the sculptor has evidently given most of his attention to the sensitive face, which has something melancholy and pathetic in its expression, but there is also a quiet dignity about it which is pleasing.

Of the conventional style of Græco-Egyptian sculpture of the Hadrianic period an example is offered by the Egyptian Antinous of the Vatican. Here nothing is Egyptian but the stiff attitude, the dress and head-dress. All the rest is Græco-Roman work, with the correct and academic modelling of body and limbs as of a Greek god or athlete. The face is a portrait of Antinous, but classicizing in style, though it clearly shows the sombre and rather heavy melancholy that is appropriate to the subject. The divine honours given by the Emperor to the favourite who died for him are more subtly expressed elsewhere. Here we have merely a Greek statue with incongruous Egyptian trappings (P. 238, fig. 2).

A different and more bizarre mixture of Roman and Egyptian elements may be seen in statuettes such as the bronze in the British Museum represented on P. 240 (fig. 1). Here the hawk-head of the Egyptian god Horus is placed upon a body clad in the panoply of a Roman general.

A branch of art in which more originality is shown may be seen in the painted portraits attached to mummy-cases (P. 242). Many have been found in the Fayum, the finest of which show both a high degree of technical skill in painting and an ability to present what is clearly an excellent and characteristic portrait. One of these is here reproduced in colour (P. 243). Sometimes the portrait is not painted, but modelled in plaster (P. 245). Such representations of the deceased on a mummy-case are in earlier times merely conventional. But these portraits, which date mostly from Roman times, probably about the second century A.D., are evidently realistic portraits, and give a vivid representation of actual features and character. It might indeed be said that there is nothing peculiarly Egyptian about them, but that they merely show us one phase of later Græco-Roman art. Nothing like this has indeed been discovered elsewhere; but though this may be partially due to conditions of preservation, they may certainly claim to be a peculiar product of Egypt. This national type is, however, more Greek than anything else, and may still be seen among the Levantine peoples.

As well as sculpture and paintings, many of the handicrafts of Egypt survived into Roman times. Glass and glazed ware produced in great quantities in the Twenty-sixth Dynasty were extensively imitated elsewhere. A mingling of Greek and Egyptian motives is often found in later times, as in the rhyton (or horn) and bowl that are shown on P. 246.

E. A. GARDNER

THE COPTIC PERIOD

CHRISTIANITY, possibly preached by St. Mark himself, was accepted rather more easily and rapidly in Egypt than in other parts of the Roman Empire, and had conquered most of the country outside Alexandria—by the middle of the third century A.D. There were two or three serious persecutions, but the new religion consolidated its position without much difficulty ; and it is important to remember the *form* which it took—monasticism. St. Anthony, the founder of Christian monasticism, lived in the century between A.D. 250 and 350, and towards the end of this time Pachomius organised the hitherto somewhat loose and undefined rules and mode of living of the monks and hermits. In the whole Christian period the leaders of religious thought are not to be found in the towns or among the Bishops (with the exception of the Patriarch of Alexandria) but in the great monasteries in the deserts on both sides of the Nile.

Artistically, it is with one exception a period of decline. It will be convenient to treat separately the various forms of art of the Christian period in Egypt, giving at the end of the chapter a brief indication of a few of the more important books on the subject (P. 60).

A. ARCHITECTURE. The Copts, or Egyptian Christians, adapted the pagan temples to their own use without doing them much damage, though they sometimes erased the paintings and reliefs or those parts of them that were near the altar. Such new buildings as they erected, in the early part of the period, were of the kind common to the Roman East ; but when they came to build the great monasteries of the deserts, they developed a style of their own, which later had some influence outside Egypt itself ; the monasteries of Baouit, of St. Jeremias at Sakkara and of St. Simeon at Assouan display a massive use of sun-dried brick (for which the Egyptian term has even, through Spanish, reached our own language in the word *adobe*), and a high vaulted arch with round top, which may have had an influence on ecclesiastical architecture in the west. They were also early inventors of the dome, the combination of which with the basilica type of building (the dome placed at one end, above the altar) formed a narthex, and this remains to this day the most characteristic type of the Eastern Christian church, and was adapted by Moslems to their own use in the construction of mosques. Of the adornment of Coptic churches, exterior and interior, I shall speak in the section on sculpture and reliefs. The architecture of the town churches follows in a modified fashion that of the monasteries, and some of those in Old Cairo preserve very early characteristics : the dome over what we should call the east end is almost universal, as opposed to the central dome of the Byzantine East.

B. SCULPTURE AND RELIEF. There was undoubtedly in Christian Egypt a fine school of ivory carving, though I profess a certain scepticism as to some pieces labelled "Egyptian" in museums : (they may have been in Egypt at some period, but their Egyptian origin appears to me doubtful). There is however no doubt about the ivory reliefs (most of them illustrating the history of St. Menas), of which the majority are in the Archæological Museum at Milan ; two, reproduced here, are in the Victoria and Albert Museum, representing part of the scene of the Miracle at Cana of Galilee and St. Peter dictating to St. Mark (above are the two words πολις ρωμη are in a thoroughly Coptic Greek script) (P. 252). These are of very high artistic merit, as is the Raising of Lazarus in the British Museum, which is equally of an early date. Rather later (perhaps even seventh or eighth century) is another ivory in the Victoria and Albert Museum : the lower panel represents the baptism of Christ by St. John, the upper shows part of the Ascension.

Ivory was only for small objects, and soon became too expensive for widespread use. Stone and wood however were freely and successfully used, and the capitals of the pillars at various monasteries display a very high standard of work; outside Egypt the best collection of them is perhaps in the new Coptic room at the Louvre, in which most of the material is from Baouit. The Coptic artists in these media were peculiarly happy in conventionalising flower and plant patterns (less often animals), and a combination of these with lace and strap work (the latter becoming more important still in the Moslem period, when religious considerations forbade the use of figures) produces a wonderfully rich effect. Reproductions are here given of a capital and of carvings and reliefs from Baouit (Pp. 247, 250 and 254), and of a wooden relief (Nativity scene) from the Church of Abu Sarga at Cairo, (P. 253, fig. 2).

C. PAINTING, ILLUMINATING, DRAWING. This is a chapter of greatly varying degrees of achievement. The early frescoes from the ruined monasteries display certain figures of a very high standard. Owing to the great destruction of church art in the Near and Middle East—the iconoclastic Moslem destroyed almost everywhere, and the rise of religious art in Russia is a late development—comparison and comparative criticism are difficult, for we have but fragmentary remains, retrieved with difficulty from beneath coats of whitewash or plaster. But if the Coptic frescoes at the monastery of St. Jeremias at Sakkara be placed alongside of the (rather later) frescoes of Constantinople, they have little to fear. The figure of Christ, at once saviour and judge, usually found in the narthex, attains a kind of sublimity, combining majesty and tenderness in a manner hardly equalled elsewhere (P. 253, fig. 1).

The Egyptian artist, as we know from the sarcophagi of the Græco-Roman period, had the power of composition and the ability to give what we call a

" likeness "—the features of the individual whose mummy is beneath are sharply characterised ; the painting is in every sense of the word a portrait. In the early Coptic period this power of individualisation is also found in the work of the fresco-painters, as will be seen in the figures of Christ mentioned above, and in those of saints in the chapels of the monastery churches, of which a good example is reproduced in " the Samaritan " and Apa Paule standing together in one of the chapels at Baouit ; in these the classical tradition, especially in the drapery, which represents the typical and traditional dress of a gentleman of the Eastern Roman Empire, is still a living thing. Decline was however rapid : the figures became stiff and stilted, and a numbing convention took away interest and life : action and movement perhaps prevailed longest in the figures of the "equestrian saints," whose figures on horseback with a lance, riding down a dragon or some heathen adversary on foot, seem to retain a certain liveliness when other contemporary work is dead. One of the few late wall-drawings (it is something between a fresco and a graffito) which escapes from conventional shackles is the picture of the Three Holy Children in the burning fiery furnace, in the British Museum. The execution is in many respects rude, but the figures, with their curious Phrygian caps and medieval—not classical—dress are living and active (P. 255).

In the illumination of manuscripts this same rather rapid degeneration is apparent. Here again the material on which to base our judgment is sadly fragmentary. Nine-tenths (perhaps more) of all extant Coptic literature has come down to us not in complete volumes but in single leaves or gatherings of a few pages : the manuscripts partly disintegrated through centuries of neglect in monasteries where nobody cared to read them ; for the best—all indeed of the period of which I am now writing—were in the southern dialect unfamiliar to the medieval Egyptian monk, whose natural idiom was Arabic, and his church language the northern dialect of Coptic ; and they were partly torn to pieces by the vandalism of dealers, who anticipated a higher profit by sales of fragments to travellers than by disposing of whole books. The Pierpont Morgan collection in New York is unique in the number of complete volumes it contains, and a study of it is indispensable to the student of Coptic literature and those branches of art which have to do with books : with princely generosity the owner has presented a complete photographic facsimile of all fifty-six volumes of the collection to five or six of the more important libraries of Europe.

The date of the manuscripts of this collection may be placed roughly in the ninth century A.D. This is later than the period of which I am generally treating in this chapter, but of the strictly Christian period we have almost no illuminations left : Coptic art was very conservative, and the pictures in the Pierpont Morgan manuscripts do not probably differ much from what we should have had three centuries before, except by being a little stiffer and more conventional. Of the earlier centuries, one of the very few manuscript illuminations that have come down to us is a drawing of Job and his three daughters, in a Coptic manuscript of the Book of Job (fifth or sixth century) in the part of the Borgia collection now at Naples (P. 256). In spite of a certain roughness of execution, the figures, and even the faces, are lively and not without expression. From the Pierpont Morgan collection I have chosen for reproduction the frontispieces of two Synaxaria dated A.D. 895 and 914 respectively : the former represents St. Stephen between two angels (he is represented as bearded and of mature years, instead of the young deacon familiar to us in the west), the latter the Annunciation ; above the figures are their descriptions in Coptic, "St. Mary the Virgin : Gabriel the Announcer," and between them in Greek the words of the angelic salutation. The artistic decline in these figures will easily be observed. The drapery is still fairly well treated, though its folds are too rigid ; but the faces have little expression, and nose and eye-brows are represented by a conventional combination of lines, which scarcely varies with the subject portrayed (P. 255).

In later times, book-illumination fell very low. Human figures became barbaric and even childish, and in the middle ages we find little but crosses and representations of the Holy Dove, the latter conventionalised and coloured so that it has more the appearance of a parrot. The last signs of life seem to me to have persisted in the former : the cross is ornamented with strap-work, sometimes of extraordinary elaboration, in red and green if colour is employed. This is a relic of a very ancient tradition in Christian Egypt, and I have been struck with the resemblance between these Coptic crosses and those found in early Celtic manuscripts   The Irish brought from Egypt the monastic idea (though they afterwards developed it on very different lines) : could they have derived this detail of artistic treatment from the same source ?

In the British Museum [MS. Or. 3367(3)] are fragments from a later manuscript—it may still be ninth or tenth century, though in the northern dialect —because it may represent what is very rare in Coptic art, external influence. The text is the Gospel of St. John : the figure with the head bent far back is probably Christ, the others doubtful, though the upper picture may be of Christ and St. Peter. The treatment is unlike that of ordinary Coptic work, and I cannot help thinking that the illuminator (a deacon, Macarius) may have seen a western manuscript. The figures are booted, and there is something in their pose, especially in the figure of Christ with head upturned, that makes me think of even an Anglo-Norman model.

D. TEXTILES. This is the only form of art in which the Christian Egyptians excelled. The pagan period is outside my survey, and though we have remains from it—and beautiful remains—it is probable that as good work was done elsewhere in the Mediterranean basin and east of it, and we owe to the Egyptian climate specimens of what has perished elsewhere.

The Copts not only carried on a noble tradition, but improved it. Here, as in certain other walks of life in Egypt, the coming Christianity made no violent break ; figures of Apollo and Hermes passed easily into representations of the saints, and the ankh, or sign of life, became a looped cross. The Coptic weavers attained a high degree of skill both in wool and silk, sometimes combining the two : and in the latter part of their period, when purity of figure-design and outline has declined, its place is taken by two other characteristics—the use of a great number of bright and intense colours in harmonious juxtaposition and the happy conventionalising of flowers, animals and other motives into patterns unrivalled except perhaps in the rugs of Persia and southern Central Asia.

In addition to woven objects, the Copts produced various forms of painted or dyed linen cloths, including some very successful " resist prints " ; but it is for their woven work that they will always be most famed. During the past hundred years a very great quantity of this has been discovered in Egyptian burying-grounds : and though most of it is fragmentary, all the more important museums of Europe and America have been able to acquire sufficient pieces for study and appreciation : uncoloured reproductions give but a poor representation of these objects, combining high technical skill with great beauty of design and tone (Pp. 259-261).

E. MINOR ARTS. Very few articles of personal adornment have come down to us from the Christian period : the Copts were so long a subject race that they lost most of their possessions of value. We have however censers and lamps, some with enamel ornament, which show that they attained a fair degree of skill in metal work : and the standard is about the same in domestic pottery, of which a good number of examples has been found in the excavation of monasteries and other sites. The pots for water-carrying do not differ greatly from their predecessors in Ancient Egypt, or those used throughout the Arab period until the coming of the kerosene tin : pottery lamps have also been found in considerable quantities, often bearing the figure of a Saint ; of a similar work were ampullæ, used to bring sacred water away from shrines (e.g. that of St. Menas in the Libyan desert). I have also thought it worth while to reproduce a pottery model which I bought some years ago from the de Rustafjaell collection and gave to the Fitzwilliam museum at Cambridge. It is probably a lamp, made in the form of a model of a church. Note the conventionalised persea trees on either side of the door (P. 262).

The monks and hermits employed such time as could be spared from prayer in weaving mats, rugs and other domestic implements from grass. We fortunately possess a fair quantity of these from Thebes.

The art of decorating leather for book-bindings was highly developed, especially in the skilful combination of crosses, circles and strap-work into elegant patterns. We have examples in the Pierpont Morgan collection of manuscripts (P. 256, fig. 2).

STEPHEN GASELEE

BIBLIOGRAPHY

A. Clédat, " Le Monastère de Baouit," " Mémoires de l'Institut français au Caire " XII, and " Comptes rendus de l'Académie des Inscriptions, 1902 and 1904."

Quibell, " Excavations at Saqqara," 1907-1910. 2 vols. Cairo, 1909 and 1912.
Winlock and Crum, " The Monastery of Epiphanius at Thebes," 2 vols. New York, 1926.
Mileham and Randall-Maciver, " Churches in Lower Nubia," Philadelphia, 1910.
Somers Clarke, " Christian Antiquities in the Nile Valley," Oxford, 1912.
Butler, " Ancient Coptic Churches of Egypt," 2 vols. Oxford, 1884.
Patricolo, " The Church of St. Barbara," Cairo, 1922.

B. The same books should be consulted as those for section A, adding Strygowski's Cairo Catalogue, " Koptische Kunst," Cairo, 1904, his " Orient oder Rom," Leipzig, 1901, and his many articles in periodicals on the same and like subjects.

C. The same books should be consulted as those for section B, adding Hyvernat's " Album de Paléographie Copte," Paris 1888, and " Check List of Coptic Manuscripts in the Pierpont Morgan Library," New York, 1919.

D. M. Gerspach, " Les tapisseries coptes," Paris, 1890. Anon., " Etoffes et tapisseries coptes," Paris (1913-14). This, a series of coloured reproductions of Coptic textiles, would have been the most important collection on this subject : it was being brought out in Paris by H. Ernst (" éditeur ") for the bookseller Hessling, but only four fasciculi had appeared at the outbreak of the Great War, and no more followed—I believe the plates were being made in Germany.

A. F. Kendrick " Catalogue of textiles from burying grounds in Egypt " (in the Victoria and Albert Museum), 3 vols. London, 1920-1922.
Laura E. Start, " Coptic Cloths " : Bankfield Museum notes, second series, No. 4. Halifax, 1914. This is a pamphlet of some importance, and too little known. The author goes deeply into the technique of Christian-Egyptian weaving, and illustrates by description—and more important, by diagram—the exact methods employed. She adds a bibliography of books on the subject up to 1914.
Volbach and Kuehnel, " Late Antique, Coptic and Islamic Textiles," London 1930.
O. von Falke, " Kunstgeschichte der Seideweberei," 2 vols. Based on Lessing's remains.
I do not give a list of the catalogues of textiles in various national collections : but I may mention, *ne pereat*, that " Barcelona-Atracción " of January, 1919, contained an illustrated description of the by no means uninteresting pieces in the Barcelona Museum ; quite a large number, and a comparatively recent acquisition.

E. Consult Winlock and Crum (Section A), Strzygowski (Section B), Hyvernat's " Check List " (Section C), and add J. C. E. Falls' " Three years in the Libyan Desert " (English translation), London, 1913, and R. de Rustafjaell, " The Light of Egypt," London, 1909, together with the catalogue of the de Rustafjaell sale, Sotheby's, January 20th, 1913.

THE MUSLIM PERIOD
I. ARCHITECTURE

ALTHOUGH the Muslim architecture of Egypt begins in the ninth century with the Nilometer and the Mosque of Ibn Tūlūn, it is quite impossible to understand these structures without a few words on the beginnings of Islam.

In the days of Muhammed the Arabs had nothing worthy of the name of architecture. The house which he built at Medīna after his migration from Mekka consisted of an open courtyard, about 60 yards square, surrounded by walls 10-11 feet high, built of dry rubble below and mud bricks above. This courtyard, which afterwards served as a place of prayer, was at first quite open, but, as the Companions complained of being exposed to the burning heat of the sun, a shelter was erected, consisting of palm trunks used as columns supporting a roof of palm-leaves and mud. At the south-east corner of the courtyard, against the outer wall, were the huts occupied by Sauda and Aisha, the wives of Muhammed, also built of mud bricks and thatched with palm-leaves. As Muhammed took other wives additional huts were constructed. All these huts opened into the courtyard. There were no lamps, and the evening devotions were accomplished by the light of a fire of palm-leaves.

At first the congregation turned towards Jerusalem when praying, a practice due to contact with the Jews, who occupied an important position in Medīna at this time. Muhammed had wished to come to a political agreement with them, but his efforts failed and he ultimately decided to break with them. The outward and visible sign of this decision was the change in the qibla or direction of prayer (January 10th, 624), which henceforth became Mekka.

After Muhammed's death in 632 a period of great campaigns opened. The advance of the Arabs was fan-wise; north-west they spread into Syria and made contact with Syro-Byzantine civilization, north-east they spread into Mesopotamia (Irāq) and Persia and made contact with the civilization of the Sasanian empire. This fact is of paramount importance for the development of Islamic architecture, as became manifest by the second half of the seventh century. The armies of Islam were composed chiefly of coarse Bedawin from the heart of eastern Arabia, knowing Muhammed and the Qur'ān merely by name, and taking part, not in a religious war for the propagation of the faith, but in the hope of gratifying their insatiable lust for loot. They had no soul for art or architecture, and like all true nomads, no wish to dwell in towns. After about two generations, when the Arabs began to settle down and to require permanent habitations, they turned to Sasanian architects on the Mesopotamian front, to Syrian architects on the Syrian.

NOTE.—The photographs illustrating this chapter are by the author, with the exception of those on pages 287 and 302.

The concave mihrāb (or niche indicating the direction of prayer), the maqsūra (or enclosure for the Caliph, or the provincial governor), and the minbar (pulpit), all of which are of non-Muslim origin, appear at the end of the seventh or the beginning of the eighth century.

In Syria most of the early mosques were converted churches, conversion being effected by closing the west entrances, by making openings in the north side, and by praying towards the south wall (i.e., towards Mekka). Hence the distinct predilection in Syria for a sanctuary with three aisles (the ancient three-aisled basilica employed transversely). In Mesopotamia, where the chief centres of Arab settlement were new foundations such as Basra and Kufa, a different type of mosque was evolved. At Basra the first mosque was simply marked out on the ground, and the people prayed there without any buildings. At Kufa the boundaries of the mosque were marked out by a man who stood on the site chosen and threw an arrow in the direction of the qibla, then another towards the north, another to the west, and a fourth to the east. A square, with each side two arrow-casts long, was thus obtained. The area was enclosed by a ditch, and the only structural part was a covered colonnade (*zulla*), open on all sides, which ran the whole length of the south side. The columns were taken from the ruins of Hīra. Against the south side was built the dwelling of the Commander-in-Chief. It is important to observe that we have here, as early as the year 638, a group—a square mosque, with the Governor's residence built against the south side—that was destined to persist for several centuries.

In A.D. 750 occurred an event which had a profound influence on Islam— the fall of the only really Arab dynasty, the Umayyad, and the rise of the 'Abbasids, who transferred the seat of government to Baghdād, which was founded by al-Mansūr in 762. This change was as fundamental as the transfer of the capital of the Roman Empire from Rome to Constantinople, the centre of gravity of the empire in each case being displaced towards the east. The influence of Syria and Byzance on Muslim art was thereby decreased, and the influence of the traditions of Sasanian Persia and Central Asia enormously increased. The first great mosque of Baghdād appears to have been about 125 yards square, with a courtyard (*sahn*) in the centre, a sanctuary five arcades deep on the qibla side, and arcades two aisles deep on the other three sides, all covered with flat roofs. From 836 to 892 the seat of the Caliphate was at Sāmarrā, about 75 miles higher up the Tigris. Here considerable remains have been preserved above ground, and an enormous quantity of stucco ornament has been recovered by the excavations of Sarre and Herzfeld. The pointed arch is found here in the ruins of the Caliph's palace (it was known still earlier in Syria).

We must now turn to Egypt, which had remained extremely backward architecturally, having been a conquered province for over two centuries,

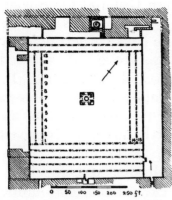

Fig. 8. The Mosque of Ibn Tūlūn

bled white for tribute under a series of extortioners, scarcely any of whom remained in office for more than three years. The Umayyad period is consequently quite unrepresented there. At last, however, Egypt became the seat of an independent ruler, Ahmad Ibn Tūlūn, who came from Sāmarrā bringing with him the architectural traditions of that great city. His mosque (Fig. 8), in plan related to that of Baghdād, in ornament to the monuments of Sāmarrā, is thus an absolutely foreign (Mesopotamian) product, planted down on the soil of Egypt. The legend of the Christian architect, invented solely to explain the use of piers (a novelty in Egypt) instead of columns, may be unhesitatingly rejected. The three types, under which Herzfeld has classified the ornament found at Sāmarrā, are all found in the mosque of Ibn Tūlūn, together with the simplest and almost the earliest examples of geometrical ornament in Islam (soffits of arches on the south-west side of the court). The whole structure is built of brick, and the slightly stilted pointed arch is employed throughout.

The FĀTIMID PERIOD (969-1171) commenced with the conquest of Egypt by Gōhar, the general of the Fātimid Caliph El-Mu'izz, in 969. From this year dates the foundation of Cairo (Al-Qāhira) on unoccupied ground to the north of Fustāt and Al-Qatā'i (the town of Ibn Tūlūn). The city was a fortified enclosure about 1,200 yards square, containing two palaces for the Caliph (a larger one on the east, and a smaller one on the west), government offices, quarters for the garrison, treasury, mint, library, imperial mausoleum, arsenal, etc. Until the fall of the Fātimid dynasty in 1171, no person was allowed to enter the walls of the city except the soldiers of the garrison and the highest officers of State. In this respect it recalls the arrangement at Peking of the Chinese City, the Tartar City, and the Forbidden City, as laid out by Qubilai Khan three centuries later.

No fragment of the enclosure remains to-day, but some carved wooden friezes from the smaller Fātimid palace are fortunately to be seen in the Museum of Arab Art. Gōhar also built a mosque, the Gāmi' al-Azhar, which was commenced in 970 and completed in the following year. Columns were used instead of piers. Though it has been much altered, it is easy to see that the original sanctuary was five aisles deep, and the side ones three, but the number on the north side remains doubtful. Its most striking feature is the transept, which runs from the sahn to the mihrāb, and against which the arcades on either side stop short. This is the first example of a transept in the mosques of Egypt, but it is found earlier in Syria, for the Great Mosque at Damascus, built by al-Walīd in 705-715, has one. It would appear that this feature was taken to the west (Great Mosque of Sidi Uqba at Qairowān, A.D. 836) and that it was brought thence to Egypt by the Fātimids. In the Azhar Mosque there was probably a dome at each of the back corners, exactly as may be seen in the Mosque of al-Hākim, built 990-1012. A detailed examination of the latter enables us to analyse its sources of inspiration. Its nearly square plan, its numerous doors, the five sanctuary aisles of seventeen arches each, the piers, and the little arches over them, which lighten the masonry, are all Mesopotamian features ; the transept is ultimately derived from Syria, as also are the entrances (now walled up) in the middle of the north-east and south-west sides (compare the Great Mosque at Damascus). The semi-fortified appearance given by the two great salients containing the minarets, and the monumental entrance repeat a scheme found in the oldest Fātimid mosque, that at Mahdia in Tunisia.

Cairo was refortified by Badr al-Gamāli in 1087-92, the town having outgrown the original enclosure. Of this new work three well-preserved gateways remain, the Bāb an-Nasr, the Bāb al-Futūh, and the Bāb Zuwayla and over 300 yards of the city wall, set with square towers. Each of these gates has a distinct individuality and is the work of a different architect, three Armenian refugees from Edessa (Urfa), which had fallen into the hands of the Seljuk Turks the previous year (1086). These gates, curtain-wall, and towers are of exceptional interest as being among the few examples remaining of Muslim military architecture prior to the Crusades. The Bāb an-Nasr is defended by a pair of machicoulis, a device in fortification not found in Europe until the end of the twelfth century. The passage-ways of the Bāb al-Futūh and the Bāb Zuwayla are covered by a shallow dome of cut stone resting on spherical-triangle pendentives of the same curvature (" calotte sur pendentifs "), the earliest example of this feature in Egypt. Practically every architectural feature of these fortifications can be traced to north Syria, and their inspiration, as fortifications, is Byzantine.

The chief glory of Fātimid architecture lay in its ornamentation, which compels universal admiration by the boldness and variety of its designs. This ornament consists of decorative writing and of arabesque patterns of a very high order, sometimes worked into a geometrical framework, sometimes not. Geometrical ornament at this time played quite a subordinate part, and the famous interlacing star pattern, which in later times had ten, twelve, or even more points, is only found in its simplest form, the eight-pointed star. Unlike the Tūlūnid period, in which Mesopotamian influences predominate, the Fātimid period is noteworthy for the beginning of Syrian influences, which later on became such a dominating feature under the Ayyubids and early Mamluks. In decorative script, Persian and north Mesopotamian influences appear to be the dominant factor, and the development of many distinctive features, such as the plaiting of the shafts of the letters, etc., is often a century in advance of Egypt in those countries. An adequate analysis of the question, however, cannot yet be made, owing to the scarcity of contemporary monuments outside Egypt, and this fact alone adds immensely to the importance of the wonderful series of Fātimid monuments preserved in Cairo.

The AYYUBID PERIOD (1171-1250) opens with the military work of Saladin, who built a great part of the present walls of Cairo, besides the mighty Citadel, which is so conspicuous an object as one approaches the city. Unfortunately none of the religious buildings erected by him in Egypt has survived. Unlike the Fātimids, who used square towers, Saladin always employed half-round towers about 20 feet wide, with two arrow slits giving a flanking, and one a forward fire. His curtain-walls at the Citadel have a continuous internal gallery 3 feet wide running through them, but his city wall is without this feature, except in the case of the east wall, where there is a short length of gallery attached to each tower.

The most noteworthy device in fortification introduced by Saladin was the bent entrance. Something of the sort seems to have been known in ancient Egypt, but Babylon, Rome, Byzance, and early Islam apparently knew it not. The Bāb al-Mudarrag at the Citadel (hidden away behind Muhammed Ali's Bāb al-Gedīd) is the earliest dated example in the Middle East (1184). The object of such an entrance is of course to break the rush of a storming party. The Bāb al-Qarāfa, on the opposite side of the Citadel, which was excavated by the writer in 1923 is another example of the same date.

Saladin's brother al-'Ādil reinforced the Citadel, in some places with great square towers, in others by building round the half-round towers and trebling their diameter, e.g. the two great towers facing 'Abbasiya. Saladin introduced the madrasa or theological school into Egypt, but the cruciform type did not appear until nearly a century later.

The Ayyubid period was therefore marked by the military architecture of Saladin, the introduction of the madrasa, the increasing use of hewn stone, the introduction of marble panelling for mihrābs (e.g. in the Mausoleum of Sultan as-Sālih Ayyub), by the development of stucco ornament in the direction of almost excessive fineness, by the first use of glass in connection with pierced stucco grilles (Mausoleum of the 'Abbasid Caliphs) and by the first steps in the evolution of the stalactite pendentive.

BAHRITE MAMLUKS (1250-1382). This period witnessed an important development in the early mosque plan, whereby the little dome which, in the Hākim Mosque for example, covers the space in front of the mihrāb, is replaced by a really large dome of wood which covers nine bays (3 by 3) and dominates the sanctuary, e.g. in the Mosque of Baybars I (at 'Abbasiya, 1269), an-Nāsir Muhammed (in the Citadel, 1318-1335), al-Māridānī (1340).

The Syrian number (three) and arrangement of the doors were also adopted. It was Baybars I, also, who introduced the stalactite portal from Syria, henceforth such a distinctive feature in the Muslim architecture of Egypt. The greatest achievement of the period was the Madrasa of Sultan Hasan (1356-1363). Its dimensions are truly colossal : in length it measures about 490 feet, and its greatest breadth is about 220 feet ; it covers an area of nearly 8,000 square yards (Fig. 9). When one stands at the entrance to the great sahn, and observes its vast proportions, its rich yet restrained decoration, the grandeur and simplicity of its lines, the height and breadth of its great vaults, and the rich stalactite balconies of the minaret rising over the south corner, one feels bound to admit that this madrasa is one of the great things of the world. Richer and more delicate monuments were built in Egypt under the following dynasty, but as an expression of power and majesty we shall never find its equal.

Faience mosaic makes its appearance for the first time in Egypt in the mosques of an-Nāsir Muhammad (1335) and Aslām al-Bahā'i (1345) and in the mausoleum of Princess Togha'i (d. 1349), doubtless introduced by the Persian architect from Tabrīz, who had built the mosque of Qūsūn in 1330. But it died out immediately, and we do not meet with any other examples of architectural faience until the end of the XVth century.

The period of the Bahrite Mamluks is marked also by the invention of the cruciform madrasa ; by the introduction of striped (*ablaq*) masonry for the decoration of façades ; by the final development and gradual extinction of stucco ornament ; and by the introduction of splendid dados of many-coloured marble.

CIRCASSIAN MAMLUKS (1382-1517). The architecture of this period follows that of the previous one without any break in development. The rich stucco decoration which had become extinct towards the end of the previous period is not immediately replaced ; at first the stone surfaces were left smooth and marble panelling was the chief enrichment, but when plastic skill in the new material was once acquired, elaborate carved surface decoration once more became a regular feature. The period is noteworthy for the last stages in the development of the stalactite pendentive ; niches are set out Syrian fashion in a triangular frame, but, unlike Syrian pendentives, each tier is curved in plan instead of cutting across the corner in a straight line ; there is a great increase in the number of tiers, seven, eight, or nine being common and even as many as thirteen being known. Domical construction culminated ; the domes of this period, which are always of stone, are without rivals for lightness, beauty of outline, and richness of decoration, a notable example being the Barqūq Mosque in the Tombs of the Caliphs. The ancient type of mosque is replaced towards the end of this period by a type of structure hitherto used for madrasas only.

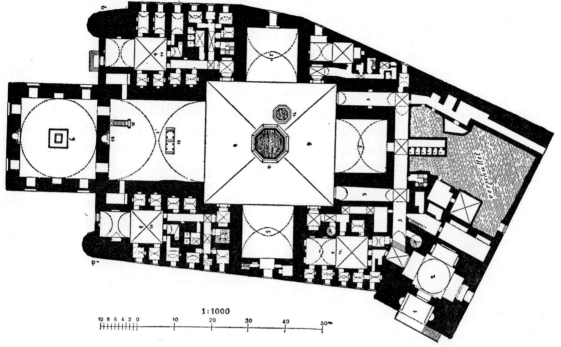

Fig. 9. The Madrasa of Sultan Hasan

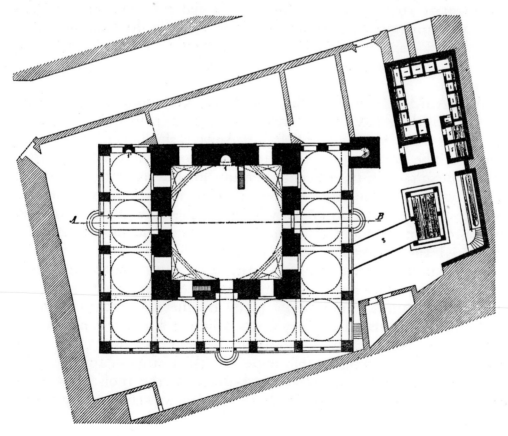

F.g. 10. The Mosque of Sinān Pasha at Būlāq

TURKISH PERIOD. The Turkish conquest in 1517 at first caused a serious diminution in every branch of industry : a large number of craftsmen were sent to Constantinople, and it is even stated that many crafts became extinct in Cairo. It has been the custom to belittle the Turkish period ; nevertheless it would appear that the enormous reduction in the amount of money hitherto spent on grandiose monuments by the rich Mamluk Court was a more serious factor than an actual falling off in the quality of work. The small mosques of Sidi Sarīya in the Citadel, Sinān Pasha at Būlāq (Fig 10), and al-Malika Safīya suffice to justify this opinion. The withering effect of European influence was destined to deal the final blow at all spontaneous self-expression in architecture, but fortunately not so soon in Egypt as elsewhere. This fatal influence, whose arrival is signalled at Constantinople by the Nuri Osmaniyc Mosque, finished about 1753, and at Damascus by a baroque fountain, built in 1798, does not appear to have reached Egypt until after 1820.

MOSQUES, the most important monuments of Islamic art, may be divided into two categories, the Gāmi' or mosque for the congregational prayer on Friday, and the Masgid or praying-place. Besides these there is the Zāwiya or small chapel. The oldest type of congregational mosque found in Egypt is of Mesopotamian origin (e.g. Ibn Tūlūn). Around a nearly square court (*sahn*) are four flat-roofed porticoes (*riwaq*). The chief riwāq, or sanctuary, placed on the side towards Mekka, has usually five aisles (Ibn Tūlūn, al-Azhar, al-Hākim) or six aisles (Baybars I), while the other sides have only two (Ibn Tūlūn) or three (al-Azhar, al-Hākim, and Baybars I).

MADRASAS. The religious, dogmatic, ceremonial, social, and moral precepts of Islam have taken form under four principal rites, founded by the Imāms Abū Hanifa, Malik ibn Anās, ash-Shafī'i, and Ahmad ibn Hanbal. The Madrasa was a kind of theological college introduced by the Seljuq Sultans in the eleventh century for the teaching of these rites, and for the training of the large body of officials needed by the Seljuq administration. As there was no hostility between the various rites, they sometimes made provision for more than one rite in the same building. Nūr ad-Dīn introduced the institution into Syria, and Saladin, after the fall of the Fātimid dynasty, carried it into Egypt, in order to combat the Shiite heresy of the Fātimids and ensure the triumph of the Sunnite reaction.

The architectural form usually taken by the madrasa in Egypt after the middle of the thirteenth century was as follows : a square central court flanked by four open halls or līwāns, forming the branches of a cross. This figure is inscribed in a rectangle, the angles of which are occupied by the dependencies, the great entrance-bay, a staircase to the roof, halls, cells for the professors, etc. In early examples the līwāns are covered by tunnel-vaults, in later examples there is merely a frontal arch with a flat timber roof behind it. The prevalence of this type gave rise to the idea that Egyptian madrasas were always built for all four rites, and the fact that the institution was introduced from Syria gave rise to the theory that the cruciform type was introduced from Syria also. Both these ideas are erroneous. We now know that although no fewer than eight madrasas built before 1270 exist in Syria, none of them has either a cruciform plan or four great līwāns, but that a cruciform madrasa was built in Egypt as early as 1263 by Sultan Baybars I, and we are therefore justified in saying that the cruciform plan was first employed for a madrasa in Egypt.

To return to the evolution of the mosque proper. The disadvantages of the arcaded type of mosque for preaching in may be realized by mounting the pulpit (say in the mosque of Ibn Tūlūn) and observing how little of the congregation would be visible from it, owing to the obstruction caused by the piers of the arcades. In the madrasa, on the contrary, one's vision of the congregation is not obstructed, and it is therefore not surprising to find that the madrasa plan gradually ousts the older plan, and that it is sometimes adopted for mosques as early as the fourteenth century (mosques of the Emir Yl-Malak, 1319, and Aslām al-Bahā'i, 1345), and frequently in the fifteenth century (Mosques of Gamāl ad-Dīn al-Ustadār, 1408 ; Gāni Bek, 1427 ; Gōhar al-Lala, 1430, Qigmas al-Ishāqi, 1481). In the last century of the Mamluk period the size of the sahn was much reduced and a skylight placed over it.

After the conquest of Egypt by the Turks in 1517, the influence of the Byzantine-Ottoman style caused the introduction of a sanctuary covered by a large dome and preceded by a court surrounded by arcades roofed with little domes (e.g. al-Malika Safīya, 1610).

INTERNAL EQUIPMENT. The centre of the court (*sahn*) was usually occupied by a fountain (*fasqiya*) under a little wooden dome resting on columns. This, however, was not for ablution, which, until after the Turkish conquest, was performed in an adjoining court. It then became usual to have a structure with taps all round (*hanafiya*) in the centre of the sahn, a practice which, in an earlier age, would have been regarded as polluting the mosque.

At the back of the sanctuary is to be found (1) the prayer-niche (*mihrab* ; not qibla, which merely means the direction of Mekka) ; (2) the pulpit (*minbar*), frequently a fine piece of cabinet-maker's work ; (3) the dikka, or platform supported on columns, on which the muballighin (assistants of the Imām or leader in prayer) repeat the genuflections, etc., at the same time being visible to the whole congregation, who are therefore enabled to keep time ; (4) the lamps and lanterns (*tannur*, a large chandelier), hanging from the ceiling.

MINARETS. The first mosques had no minarets, the call to prayer being given from the roof. The first minaret of Ibn Tūlūn's mosque was apparently a spiral copied from the minaret of the Great Mosque at Sāmarrā. (The present minaret was built by Lagin in 1296). In the eleventh century we find a tall square shaft surmounted by a little domed kiosk (al-Guyūshi, 1085). This little kiosk becomes more and more elaborate, its cap becoming fluted and its lower part drawn out to such an extent that eventually the minaret becomes three-storied, successively square, octagonal, and circular (e.g. the Mosque of Sangar al-Gāwlī, 1303). This evolution is so clear and so gradual that the Pharos theory of the origin of the minaret must be given up. After 1340 the prevailing type consisted of an octagonal shaft, with a little domed kiosk at the summit (al-Māridānī Mosque, 1340, Sheikhun Mosque, 1355).

The Mausoleums of Sultans and Emirs are generally, though not invariably, built as annexes to mosques or madrasas founded by them. The actual subterranean chamber containing the body or bodies is destitute of decoration. The corpse, wrapped in white cotton cloth, is placed with the face towards Mekka. In the chamber above the vault stands a cenotaph. This chamber is almost invariably square and covered by a dome, the transition to which from the square ground-plan provides a most interesting study for architects. The earliest Moslem domes in Egypt (Mosques of al-Hākim and al-Guyūshi) rest on semi-domed niches (known as squinches), which are placed in the corners of the square below the dome. The square is thereby converted into an octagon, on which it is easy to set a dome. In the first departure from this scheme the octagon is formed, not by a squinch, but by three niches surmounted by one (Mausoleum of al-Ga'fari and Sayeda Ātika, c. 1125). The next step was to fill the blank space on either side of the upper niche with another one, thus producing a pendentive of two tiers of three niches (Mausoleum of the 'Abbasid Caliphs, 1242-43). The next step occurs in the Mausoleum of Sultan as-Sālih Ayyub (1250), which has a comparatively large dome. Here apparently, it was felt that a more gradual transition was necessary. The earlier procedure was repeated; just as the squinch was shrunk into the corner, so we now find a pendentive, modelled on that of the 'Abbasid Caliphs, shrunk into the corner, and the final transition effected by a row of four niches placed above it. The next step was to make the pendentive of four tiers of stalactites (Mausoleum of Baybars II, al-Gashankīr, 1306-9). Five tiers first appear in the Mausoleum of the Emir Sarghatmish (1356). This type must have been evolved in Egypt, as the Syrian type is constructed quite differently, the tiers of niches, instead of being curved in plan, run straight across the corners, and are really nothing more than blind niches carved on tiers of oversailing lintels. Moreover the number of niches in each tier is generally more or less equal in Egypt, while in Syria there is only one in the lowest tier, two in the next, and so on.

PALACES. Of the ancient Palaces, several fortunately remain, but none earlier than the middle of the fourteenth century. The ground-floors are of good solid masonry entirely vaulted, but the ceilings of the first floor are almost invariably of timber painted and gilded, and sometimes beautifully coffered, as in the Palace of the Emir Beshtāk (d. 1341). Projecting balconies were also a feature.

DWELLING-HOUSES rarely had more than two storeys. On the ground-floor is the Salamlik, or men's apartments, and on the first floor the Harīm, or women's apartments and rooms for the family.

The chief decoration of the façade is provided by exquisite mashrabīya balconies. During the last thirty years it can scarcely be an exaggeration to say that 90 per cent. of these have disappeared, and the streets of Cairo have thereby lost their most distinctive cachet. Perhaps the best vista to be seen to-day is in the street which runs west from the madrasa of Gamāl ad-Dīn, skirting the Beshtāk Palace, and comes out into the Sharia Bayn as-Surayn.

The following rules are generally observed in the construction of a house. (1) The principal rooms face north (direction of the prevailing wind) and look into the court. (2) The windows looking on to the street are few and placed high. (3) The passage leading from the street to the court is built with a right-angled turn to prevent passers-by from seeing into the court. (4) The entrance to the harīm is placed in a second court, or on the far side of the first court. (5) The reception rooms of the master of the house, servants' quarters, kitchen, etc., are arranged round the first court.

A Wakala (or Wikala, storehouse, caravanserai), commonly called Okāla, is frequently a very large building, several storeys high, with a courtyard in the centre. The ground floor on the exterior consists of a number of rooms open to the street, which are let out as shops. Above are living quarters, let out to passing merchants or permanent residents. A monumental gateway in the centre of the façade leads to the courtyard, round which are store rooms for merchandise, with living quarters above, frequently served by outer galleries or balconies, running all round. These buildings, warehouses and tenements in one, were a form of investment before the days of limited liability companies, and benefactors, wishing to endow a mosque or madrasa, frequently built okālas, the rents derived from them being administered by trustees. Such an arrangement is called a Waqf.

The neglect from which the study of the Moslem architecture of Egypt has hitherto suffered is chiefly due to the rival glamour of the immensely old monuments of ancient Egypt. There are few visitors, however, who can fail to be thrilled by the charm of Islamic art, the splendid façades of the fourteenth and fifteenth centuries, the beautiful forms of its innumerable domes and minarets, and the extraordinary refinement of its ornament.

K. A. C. CRESWELL

MUSLIM PERIOD
II. APPLIED ARTS

MAGNIFICENT and impressive as is the architecture of Muslim Egypt, these monuments constitute only one expression of the artistic activity of this age, so fruitful in works of art. Movable objects, however, being fashioned of materials less enduring and more exposed to the forces of destruction, have survived in fewer numbers and are for the most part to be found scattered at the present time in museums and in a few private collections. For, naturally, objects made of wood, paper, silk or linen, were less durable than monumental structures of stone and marble ; even metal utensils ran the risk of being broken up, and, out of the enormous quantities of which we have historical records in the pages of the Arab historians, only comparatively few examples have survived.

In Egypt, as in all Islamic countries, no art has been so much honoured or so assiduously cultivated as that of calligraphy. Whether in architecture or in the minor arts of domestic ornament, the highly decorative Arabic script was applied to all materials used, stone, plaster, wood, metal, ceramics, glass, textiles, etc. Calligraphy attained this position of high honour on account of its association with the Quran. For not only was the copying of the word of God considered in itself as a meritorious performance, so much so that some of the most powerful sovereigns in Islam engaged personally in such pious work, but no care and expense was regarded as too great for the preparation of fine copies.

The best paper procurable, often polished by hand, was placed at the disposal of the copyist. The ink was prepared with especial care, as described in treatises that have come down to us, and gold was often used, not only for purposes of decoration, but also for shaping individual letters. Indeed in certain sumptuous examples the whole volume was copied out in letters of gold for a prince who was willing to undertake such lavish expenditure.

The history of the various forms of the Arabic script exemplified in copies of the Quran is a very lengthy and elaborate one, and the biographers who record the fame of the calligraphers make mention of the particular form or forms of writing for which each of them was particularly distinguished. In architecture and decoration, the early writing seen on seventh century tombstones developed into the majestic Kufic writing, so called because it is said to have originated from the town of Kufa in Mesopotamia. By the eleventh and twelfth centuries this had attained great decorative beauty, with its straight vertical lines standing out against a background of lovely arabesques. Saladin introduced the Syrian Naskhy, easier to read when not too intricately interlaced, and this was henceforth used for historical inscriptions, though Kufic continued to be used for Quranic or purely decorative purposes.

Several of the Qurans produced in Egypt, especially those for which the massive Quran stands described below were made, were of great size, with a page measuring in one instance at least as much as 44 by 35 inches.

The illumination of these manuscripts corresponded in magnificence and grandeur with the stately format of the volume. Special care was often devoted to the opening pages, which were decorated with arabesques and geometrical patterns in gold and various colours, among which blue was a very favourite choice, and other colours appeared in skilful combination and harmony (P. 304).

Such a volume received a binding befitting the precious character of its contents and the elaborate tooling and leather work to be found on the covers of some of the Qurans give to these volumes a high place among the achievements of the bookbinder's art.

The study of these beautiful bindings and decorated pages reveals the fact that those designs, in their amazing multiplicity, are nevertheless similar to those used for domestic decoration in an infinite number of different materials. The earliest of them to be found in architecture were engraved with a sharp instrument in plaster before it hardened.

As in the case of most other workable materials, wood also served the calligrapher to show his skill in artistic reproductions of verses from the Quran, and in historical inscriptions. Wood was not a plentiful material in Egypt; there were skilful wood carvers, however, who produced remarkable works of art, each period being represented by characteristic examples. Tulunid (ninth century) specimens display bold motives, with a curved surface. In Fatimid times, Persian influence can be detected in the beautiful panels with hunting and revelry scenes worked for a Khalif's palace, and afterwards discovered in a late thirteenth century building with their faces to the wall, the backs having been used as ordinary boards when the palace was destroyed and the materials used again (P. 306).

Very similar designs have been found on small panels of ivory, a material that might have been expected to be much used in Egypt and of which surprisingly few examples occur.

In the case of wood work, Egypt produced a characteristic use of this material in the Mashrabîya. This is a form of wooden lattice work which derives its name from one of the purposes to which it was devoted, as providing a place screened from the direct rays of the sun, yet accessible to every current of air in which porous water vessels might be kept cool. Such lattice work filled an even more important place in domestic architecture, as providing light and air for the occupants of a house in such a manner that they could look out upon the outer world while remaining invisible to the passers-by, or even to their immediate neighbours on the opposite side of the street ; the hard sunlight was filtered through this lattice work and passed into the interior chambers of the house in a softened form, agreeable and pleasant to the eye ; at the same time ample ventilation was provided without the necessity of opening either large doors or windows (P. 311).

There are unfortunately very few examples left of streets decorated with these latticed windows, which gave a peculiar and characteristic charm to the city of Cairo, and are now being replaced by very common-place casements. The structure of this lattice work was very varied in character, but the most attractive examples are made of small pieces of turned wood, arranged in squares, or diagonally, in a great variety of patterns. Even the separate little sections of wood vary considerably in shape, being either square, spherical, or even oval.

Mashrabîya work was most frequently found as applied to domestic architecture in the manner described above, but impressive examples are also found in some of the monumental tombs in Cairo in the form of railings surrounding the cenotaph.

The Cairene workers in wood exercised their ingenuity on many other objects, and among those their skill found its highest form of expression in the elaborately designed pulpits, several of which still survive (P. 310) ; one dating from the reign of Qâit-bây is preserved in the Victoria and Albert Museum in South Kensington.

Here on the main structure of wood, wooden panels, the surfaces of which are delicately carved, are inserted among diagonally arranged strips of the same material in an infinite variety of geometrical patterns. Sometimes emphasis is given to the designs by the employment of narrow lines of ivory, which follow the outline of the inset panels or present separate patterns of their own on the surface of the wood. Or else, finely carved ivory panels are inserted into the geometrical stars from which the pattern seems to start. These geometrical patterns worked in wood may have been in use in Egypt before the Muslim conquest ; they are to be seen in Coptic buildings of uncertain date, and also in other parts of North Africa.

Each one of the above-mentioned pulpits has an imposing door at its entrance, and the two flaps of the door are covered with the same elaborate decoration as is lavished on the sides of the structure.

In most of the mosques of Cairo the Mihrab, or prayer niche, is either made of the same material as the general structure itself, or receives decoration in the form of chiselled stucco, marble mosaic, or carved stone. Even here wood was sometimes employed, and in the Arab museum there is among others a fine example of a movable or " summer " mihrab entirely constructed of carved wood and dating from the twelfth century (P. 308).

Another article of the furniture of a mosque which gave the wood carver opportunities of displaying his skill was the dikka (sometimes called Kursy), or raised structure on which was placed one of those enormous copies of the Quran described above, a flat space in front of the Quran rest being provided for the reader of the sacred volume to sit cross-legged. The sides and end of this bulky structure afforded broad spaces for geometrical decoration of inlaid wood, or of wood combined with ivory just as did the sides of the pulpit.

The name of Kursy was also given to octagonal stands in wooded marqueterie of which the Arab museum possesses several charming examples. Similar pieces of furniture exist in metal work, bronze or brass inlaid with silver and even gold, a technique imported from Mosul in the twelfth and thirteenth centuries.

Fatimid metal objects are usually of moulded and engraved bronze, without any inlay, and very frequently assumed the shape of birds or animals. Of such were the utensils in the palace of the Khalif Al Mustansir, of which lists are given comprising literally thousands of metal objects of various uses. Such metal objects must have existed in very large numbers in private houses and palaces as well as in the palace of the ruler himself, but only very few early examples have survived to this day. Moreover the Fatimid empire comprised at one time such a large area that one cannot be sure whether certain objects of definite Fatimid date were not manufactured in Sicily or in North Africa (Pp. 312 and 313).

These bronze objects were superseded in Mamluk times by beautiful inlaid brass pieces such as were manufactured in Persia and then in Mosul until Tartar hordes drove craftsmen to find refuge in Egypt (thirteenth and fourteenth centuries). Once in Cairo, however, they somewhat modified their style in accordance with the fashions prevailing at the Mamluk Court, and inscriptions in tall, harmonious characters assumed a leading part in the decoration (Pp. 316—323).

Many fine pieces have been treasured in museums and private collections ; perhaps the finest are those that have been preserved on account of their associations with sacred buildings, such as mosques or tombs. Chief among the objects that have served such pious uses are the metal cases for containing a Quran divided into sections, each separately bound for the convenience of readers who undertake on an occasion of special solemnity, especially the commemoration of the death of some distinguished personage, to read through the whole Quran, and thus are able to divide the sections among several readers (P. 325, fig. 2.).

Among other objects having similar pious associations are the massive candlesticks set up one on each side of the mihrab for use in the religious services which are held at night throughout the month of Ramadan or other occasions (P. 323), and the magnificent perforated bronze or silver-inlaid brass chandeliers which hung from the dome over the tomb of the founder in funerary chapels (P. 324). The doors of mosques and of the tombs of Sultans were often covered with plates and bosses of metal, richly carved and chiselled and set together in highly complicated patterns, interspersed with quotations from the Quran, engraved on similar metal plates, or inscriptions recording the name and title of the sovereign who caused the work to be made (P. 315).

Metal objects for domestic use did not enjoy the protection of similar religious associations and have consequently survived in smaller numbers, but they include the incense burners (P. 317), bowls, dishes and other domestic utensils (Pp. 316, 318 and 321) of which many beautiful examples are to be seen in museums and private collections. Modern Egyptian craftsmen still execute similar inlaid brass work with extraordinary skill.

Any complete account of Egyptian textiles of the Muslim period would require a separate volume, for their history extends from the period immediately following the conquest in the seventh century down to comparatively recent times. The arts of weaving and embroidering were at a high level in Egypt under Byzantine rule, a level probably attained in much earlier times. Indeed it is not surprising that the fine Egyptian workers should have welcomed the importation of designs, Mesopotamian, Sassanian, Chinese, etc., which gave fresh scope to their amazing technical skill. For the knowledge of the greater part of those textiles we are dependent upon fragments that have been recovered from graves or rubbish heaps and, in the latter case, it is often very difficult to discriminate between Coptic or early Muslim work. Historians have left us descriptions, often quoted, of the weaving works at Fostât, in the island of Tinnis, and in other parts of Egypt, where linen was woven into such a delicate fabric that a whole turban length of it could be threaded through a finger ring. The Fatimid Khalifs and later the Mamluk Sultans kept up royal workshops in which materials were specially woven with royal names and titles. These workshops, as well as the textiles they produced, were called tiraz, a Persian word of which the original meaning, "embroidery," developed into "a strip of embroidered inscription " and finally into " a band of inscription," in which sense it was even applied to architectural friezes (Pp. 326 and 327).

Several fragments, of the highest historical importance, now in the Arab museum and in the Benakis and Newberry collections, bear the name of early Fatimid Khalifs and were undoubtedly manufactured in the royal Tiraz. Some of them are woven, others embroidered in silk or wool on a linen background. Besides the somewhat rare specimens of historical inscriptions, a great many fragments are to be found with a " tiraz " of a few words, such as blessings or invocations, endlessly repeated, especially in the woven specimens. Later, as is also the case in ceramics, meaningless signs are arranged to look like an inscription, either in Kufic or Naskhy characters. Some heraldic designs, such as the renowned Lion, or Panther, of Sultan Bibars, are also to be found. An interesting fragment in Professor Newberry's collection shows not only this badge but a rudimentary fleur-de-lis astonishingly like that seen in an ancient Egyptian textile in the same collection.

It may be assumed that the robes of honour that the Sultans were in the habit of bestowing upon their officials and servants as symbols of royal favour were made of these costly embroideries on woollen or silk fabrics, or of woven brocades, but similar designs were applied by a printing process to linen or cotton cloths worn by humbler persons. The latter material was, as is well known, imported into the whole of the east from India, about the fourteenth century, and several printed fragments in Mr. Newberry's collection would seem from their designs to date from that period. The printing was done by blocks or stencils, a " resist " of wax, ashes or glue being applied before dyeing ; several of these implements, found at Fostât, are now in the Cairo Arab museum ; prepared work, with paper patterns, has also been found. The colours were usually red, blue, violet and slate, each in several shades. With the advent of the Turkish regime, embroideries in Turkish style and technique were adopted by Egyptian workers, and a great many specimens of towels finely decorated in silk and gold thread, or rich velvet hangings embossed with gold and silver, were actually made in Egypt. The gorgeous embroidered panels, until quite recently manufactured yearly for the Kaaba in Mekka, as also the wonderful hand-woven Kiswa itself, constitute a proof that skilled craftsmanship in Egypt has not yet utterly deteriorated.

THOMAS ARNOLD

III. CERAMICS AND GLASSWARE

DURING the Mussulman period Egypt had reason to be proud of its amazing production of ceramics, while the decorative schemes and technical processes appear to have been as varied as the dynastic changes that took place in the country. The most remarkable objects, which by their qualities stand out from amongst the innumerable broken fragments of glass and pottery collected from the excavations of Fustat, reveal to us the three great flourishing epochs in the arts and economic prosperity, familiar to all those who have studied Egyptian history. But whether we consider the ephemeral Tulunid sovereignty, the prestigious Fatimid Kaliphate, or the peculiar rule of the Bahri Mamluks, we cannot speak with certainty of a continuous and purely Egyptian style in ceramics, although the pottery industry always flourished in the country.

It seems impossible to determine exactly the nationality of the artists ; we cannot, *a priori*, deny that native artists participated in it, for it would be futile to assert without proof that the Egyptians were no ceramists, seeing that they were past-masters in the arts of weaving and wood-carving. But in these two branches of art, as may be gathered from numerous examples, the date of which can easily be ascertained, and from a study of the technique, which remained more or less the same, the continuity of native workmanship is beyond doubt. In the case of ceramics, on the contrary, the styles appear and disappear with a rhythm as abrupt as that of the political convulsions, which leads us to believe that the successive masters of Egypt brought with them not only their armies and the great officers of their Courts, but also their master-craftsmen, whilst the ordinary artisans and workmen may have been natives, as were the scribes in the administrative departments.

A remarkable fact is that notwithstanding the great number of Egyptian specimens, whether intact or fragmentary, which have come down to our times, not a single one bears the name of a sovereign. Only some common pottery of the fourteenth century recalls the names of a few obscure Court officials.

Ibn Tūlūn imported into Egypt Mesopotamian traditions, particularly from Samarra which was during part of the nineteenth century the "Windsor" of the Kaliphs of Baghdad. The ceramics of that period resemble those of the Court of Iraq ; they show, on a white or cream background light-yellow, brown or reddish, lustre decoration, conventional, even when they represent life, and can be said to have been imported from the east, showing us indisputable examples of the high artistic life and masterful intellectual influence of the Persians.

We come across this influence again during the following century under the Fatimids, although it is also possible during that period to trace the effects of the Byzantine revival to which the Comnenes have given their name. The mingling of these two conceptions has given us works which are truer to life, more vivid and arresting than at any other period in the history of Egypt under the Muslims. Art during the Fatimid period is of an astounding splendour ; there is life and feeling in marked contrast to the severe marble decorations and starred polygons of the later periods. The faiences show great freedom of form ; we have great pot-bellied vases or deep cups like craters. They shine with incomparable splendour ; and the ever changing shades and tints of their metallic lustre surprised and delighted the traveller, Nasir-i-Khusrou, and we can well believe the glowing terms in which this Persian described the profusion and the quality of the lustred Egyptian faiences. The most frequent decorative subjects are lifelike human beings or animals ; gay scenes of musicians, drinkers and dancing girls.

We come across two signatures, two Muslim names, " Said " and " Muslim," without any other indication of their nationality. But they can the better be regarded as Egyptians in that we must attribute to the Christians of the country, the Copts, certain pieces of the same period, the decoration of which has been inspired by Christian Iconography, as for instance the severe and majestic head of Christ, represented on a fragment in the Arab museum at Cairo (P. 332). This is quite in accordance with historical data. The Fatimid period, from a political point of view, represents actually the Golden Age for the Christians, whether Copts or Armenians.

The fourteenth century, which was a period of unheard of economic prosperity, offers us an astounding number of ceramic pieces which it would be difficult properly to classify. Excavations have brought to light a profusion of objects imported from Spain, Italy, Persia, China, and if Egyptian potters drew little inspiration from European works, they undoubtedly imitated the technique of Persian faiences, particularly from Sultanabad, as also that of Chinese faiences and Celadons. The decoration of these Mamluk pieces presents an extreme variety, although, generally, the touch is colder than during the preceding periods, owing to the subject matter and to the manner of treatment ; human figures are very rare, animals are frozen in poses reminiscent of heraldry, while floral ornaments are conventional. The fashion is for a new technique, that of an engraved and under-glaze decoration whereof the tones are uniformly green or brown.

Some thirty different signatures of craftsmen are not sufficient to give us certainty ; the most frequent of these is that of a certain Ghaibi, and we find it in particular on broken fragments so different in quality that we are almost led to suppose that it must be the mark of a firm, rather than the individual signature of an artist.

Towards the end of the fifteenth century we come across mural ceramic, generally in two colours, white and blue, with floral and epigraphic decoration, but it never reached the splendour of the ceramics of Asia Minor or Syria ; nevertheless it seems certain that the conquest of Egypt by the Turks arrested its development.

To the excavations carried out at Fustat, we also owe a priceless collection of filters of water jugs in unglazed pottery. The extremely fine decoration of these filters reminds us of lace tracery, and shows geometrical designs, foliages, bands of writing, animals, groups, human beings, these latter rather crudely treated (Pp. 340 and 341).

Rock-crystals have almost disappeared from the East and the splendid pieces preserved in the museums of Europe must have crossed the Mediterranean at an early date. Two of them, justly famous, a ewer in the Treasury of Saint Mark at Venice, a Crescent at the museum of Nuremberg, bear the names of Fatimid Kaliphs, which induces us to attribute to Egypt a large share in this great industry. The testimony of a contemporary writer confirms that rock-crystal was imported from the Maghreb or from some region along the Red Sea, and cut and worked in Cairo.

The ornaments of the ewers generally represent animals treated in high relief, such as lions, leopards, panthers and various kinds of birds. A striking fact is that all the objects which have been preserved date from this same period of the tenth and eleventh centuries, although, according to experts, they continued to be popular in Egypt until the fourteenth century, when brass work inlaid with gold and silver displaced the rock-crystals.

Enamelled glassware is represented by pieces decorated with exuberant imagination and astounding richness of brilliant enamels; the outside surface of the glass, generally gilt, bears Quranic or historical inscriptions, in blue enamel rendered more attractive still by floral designs in red, green, yellow and white tones. The pieces which are intact fall into two principal series : bottles with a large body and a long thin neck, and mosque lamps. These latter have a wide opening in the shape of a funnel with underneath a wide body mounted on a double or on a single foot. Some of them which are particularly admirable appear to be enveloped in a continuous intricacy of flowers and foliage, picked out and entrenched with gold on a background of blue enamel. Of all the Muslim works of art, enamel glassware conveys an irresistible impression of light and of joy.

Most of these lamps were wrought for Sultans or Egyptian Court officials, and can with very few exceptions be attributed to the fourteenth century. We can ignore the preceding periods in respect of which the evidence may have disappeared, but it is clear that by the fifteenth century these splendid pieces had almost ceased to be made. During this latter period occurred financial crises disastrous for the Kingdom of Egypt, and culminating in an immense catastrophe, the discovery of the route to the Cape of Good Hope. No historian formally attributes to Egypt the origin of the enamelled glassware industry, inasmuch as other centres are known to us ; as for instance at Aleppo, Hebron, Tyre and Damascus in Syria Two considerable events, the expulsion of the Crusaders, in 1291, and the invasion of Tamerlain, in 1400, have the double advantage of helping us to understand the splendour of this art in the fourteenth century, and of locating it in Syria. The most attractive hypothesis would be to place this industry in Damascus itself, before the Mogul Conqueror deprived it of its artists. On the other hand, numerous inventories of the Treasures of the Court of the Kings of France very often mention glassware called Damascus glassware.

Photo, Dell & Wainwright

SEATED STEATOPYGOUS FEMALE FIGURE IN CLAY
BRITISH MUSEUM

PREDYNASTIC

PREDYNASTIC AGE	--3300 B.C.
FIRST DYNASTY	
SECOND DYNASTY	3300 —2980 B.C.

Photos, Dell & Wainwright

PREDYNASTIC CLAY ANIMALS   ASHMOLEAN MUSEUM, OXFORD

1. IVORY HUMAN FIGURINE FROM
MAHASNA   CAIRO MUSEUM

Photo by courtesy of the Egypt Exploration Society

Photo, Dell & Wainwright

2   BASALT HUMAN FIGURE
ASHMOLEAN MUSEUM, OXFORD

Photo, Dell & Wainwright

3. LAPIS LAZULI FIGURINE FROM HIERACONPOLIS
ASHMOLEAN MUSEUM, OXFORD

Photo, Dell & Wainwright

1. IVORY HEAD FROM HIERACONPOLIS
ASHMOLEAN MUSEUM, OXFORD

Photo, Dell & Wainwright

2. LIMESTONE HEAD FROM HIERACONPOLIS
ASHMOLEAN MUSEUM, OXFORD

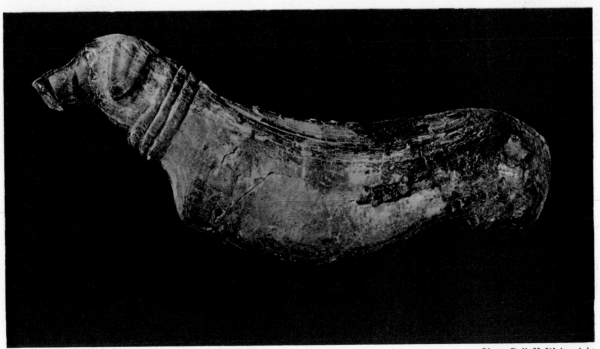

Photo, Dell & Wainwright

3. IVORY FIGURE OF A DOG FROM HIERACONPOLIS   ASHMOLEAN MUSEUM, OXFORD

Photo by courtesy of Propyläen-Verlag, Berlin

ARAGONITE FIGURE OF AN APE, BEARING THE
NAME OF KING NARMER. 20¼ ins. high. BERLIN

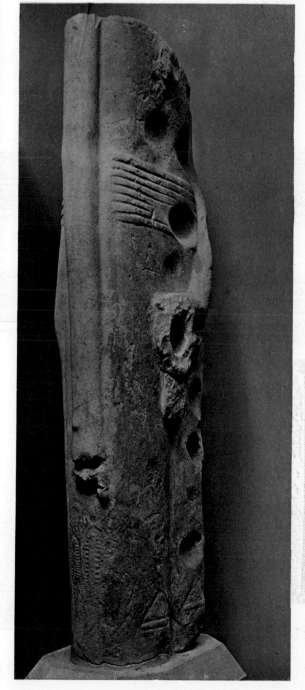

STATUE OF THE GOD MIN OF COPTOS
ASHMOLEAN MUSEUM, OXFORD

The height of this statue is
about four times that of the Ape.

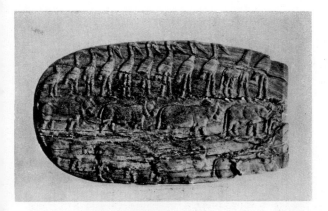 

1. IVORY KNIFE-HANDLE   METROPOLITAN MUSEUM, NEW YORK

2. IVORY FIGURINE OF A KING FROM ABYDOS   BRITISH MUSEUM

By courtesy of the Egypt Exploration Society

3. IVORY COMB

4. SLATE PALETTE. UPPER PORTION, ASHMOLEAN MUSEUM, OXFORD
LOWER PORTION, BRITISH MUSEUM
By courtesy of the Egypt Exploration Society

1. IVORY KNIFE-HANDLE FROM GEBEL 'ARAQ   LOUVRE

Photo, Dell & Wainwright

2. SLATE PALETTE FROM HIERACONPOLIS   ASHMOLEAN MUSEUM, OXFORD

MACE HEAD OF THE SCORPION KING   ASHMOLEAN MUSEUM. OXFORD

STELA OF THE SERPENT KING   CAIRO MUSEUM

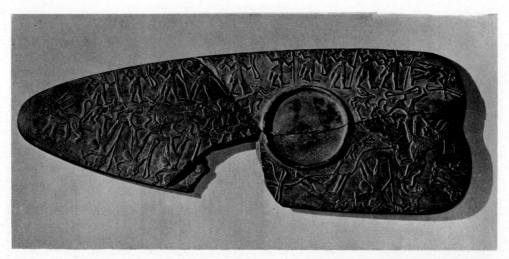

Photos, Dell & Wainwright

2. SLATE PALETTE   BRITISH MUSEUM

The upper portion on the right is restored by a cast.

STELA OF THE SERPENT KING   LOUVRE

EARLY DYNASTIC GRANITE DOOR-SOCKET
REPRESENTING A CAPTIVE ENEMY

UNIVERSITY MUSEUM
PHILADELPHIA

PREDYNASTIC POTTERY
ASHMOLEAN MUSEUM, OXFORD

1. WHITE DESIGNS ON RED

2. RED DESIGNS ON BUFF

Photos, Dell & Wainwright

1. Diorite bowls.
   Ashmolean Museum,
   Oxford.
2. 3. Pottery vases: red
   designs on buff.
   British Museum.
4. Stone vases.
   Ashmolean Museum,
   Oxford.
5. Stone vases.
   British Museum.

PREDYNASTIC POTTERY AND STONE VASES

Photo, Dell & Wainwright

Photo. Dell & Wainwright

1. PREDYNASTIC FAIENCE FIGURES   ASHMOLEAN MUSEUM, OXFORD

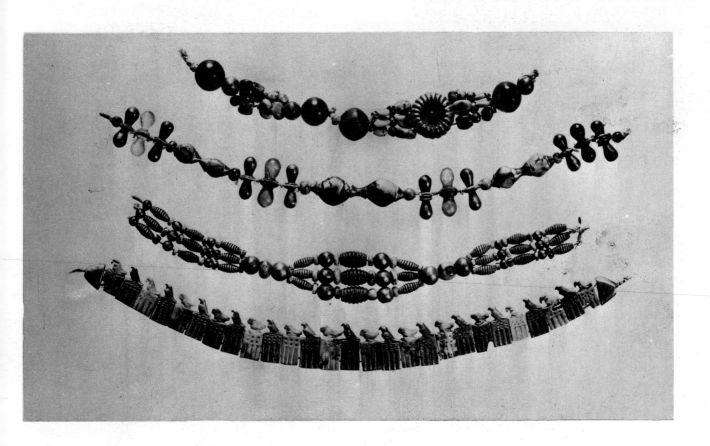

2. THE FOUR BRACELETS OF KING ZER   CAIRO MUSEUM

Photo, Exclusive News Agency

1. UNDERGROUND TEMPLE OF KHA'FRA' WITH THE SPHINX AND GREAT PYRAMID (KHUFU) BEYOND DYNASTY IV

Photo, Ricke

2. STEP PYRAMID OF ZOSER AT SAKKARA DYNASTY III

Photo, Egypt Travel Bureau

3. PYRAMID OF SNEFERU AT MĒDŪM DYNASTY IV

4. MAṢṬABA CEMETERY AT GĪZAH WITH THE PYRAMID OF KHA'FRA' BEYOND DYNASTY IV

Photo, Ricke

OLD KINGDOM

FIRST DYNASTY }	3300—2980 B.C.
SECOND DYNASTY }	
THIRD DYNASTY	2980—2900 B.C.
FOURTH DYNASTY	2900—2750 B.C.
FIFTH DYNASTY	2750—2600 B.C.
SIXTH DYNASTY	2600—2475 B.C.

SOUTHERN COLONNADE OF THE TEMPLE BUILDINGS SURROUNDING ZOSER'S PYRAMID AT SAḲḲARA
DYNASTY III   One of the remarkable imitation doors is shewn in the foreground

FAÇADE OF THE CHAPEL OF THE PRINCESS HETEP-HER-NEBTI IN THE PYRAMID AREA
OF ZOSER AT SAĶĶARA
DYNASTY III

(Restoration)

By courtesy of the Director-General, Antiquities Service, Cairo

Photo, Dell & Wainwright

2. SIDE OF AN IVORY BOX IN THE FORM
OF THE FAÇADE OF A HOUSE
BRITISH MUSEUM

3. INTERIOR OF THE TOMB OF AN
OFFICIAL NAMED SHEY; SAĶĶARA
DYNASTY VI
By courtesy of the Director-General, Antiquities Service, Cairo

4. DRAWING OF A DOORWAY IN A ROYAL TOMB
AT SAĶĶARA, WITH MISSING TILES REPLACED
DYNASTY III
By courtesy of the Director-General, Antiquities Service, Cairo

1. TWO SCULPTOR'S MODELS. LEFT, THE TITLES OF A KING.
RIGHT, PORTRAIT OF A KING WEARING THE RED CROWN
DYNASTY III. METROPOLITAN MUSEUM OF ART, NEW YORK

Photo, Dell & Wainwright

2. PORTRAIT STATUE OF KING KHA'SEKHEMUI   3. PORTRAIT STATUE OF ZOSER FROM HIS SERDAB
DYNASTY III. ASHMOLEAN MUSEUM, OXFORD   AT SAKKARA   DYNASTY III   CAIRO

Photo, Dell & Wainwright

1. BLACK GRANITE STATUE OF A NOBLEMAN
DYNASTIES II—III   BRITISH MUSEUM

2. GRANITE PORTRAIT STATUE OF AN OFFICIAL
DYNASTY III   LOUVRE

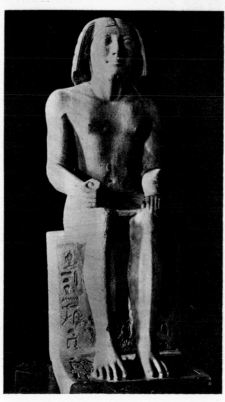

Photo, Dell & Wainwright

3. LIMESTONE PORTRAIT STATUE OF AN OFFICIAL
THENTI   DYNASTY IV   LOUVRE

4. GRANITE STATUE OF THE "SHIP-BUILDER," BEDJA
DYNASTY III   BRITISH MUSEUM

100

DIORITE STATUE OF KHA'FRA'
DYNASTY IV

CAIRO MUSEUM

GROUP IN SCHIST REPRESENTING MEN-KAU-RAʿ BETWEEN HATHOR AND A GODDESS
IMPERSONATING THE APHRODITOPOLITE NOME IN UPPER EGYPT
DYNASTY IV   CAIRO MUSEUM

PAINTED LIMESTONE STATUES OF RA'HETEP AND HIS WIFE NOFRET
DYNASTY IV

CAIRO MUSEUM

LIMESTONE STATUE OF PRINCE HEMÔN FROM GÎZAH
DYNASTY IV   PELIZAEUS MUSEUM, HILDESHEIM

ALABASTER STATUETTE

OF A PRINCESS

DYNASTY IV

BRITISH MUSEUM

Photo, Dell & Wainwright

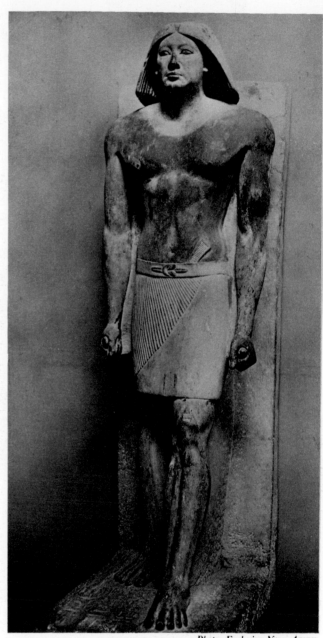

1

2

1. WOODEN STATUE FROM A TOMB AT SAKKARA
KNOWN AS THE SHEIKH EL-BELED
DYNASTY V   CAIRO MUSEUM

2. PAINTED LIMESTONE STATUE OF RA·NEFER

DYNASTY V   CAIRO MUSEUM

PAINTED LIMESTONE STATUE OF A SEATED SCRIBE
DYNASTY V

LOUVRE

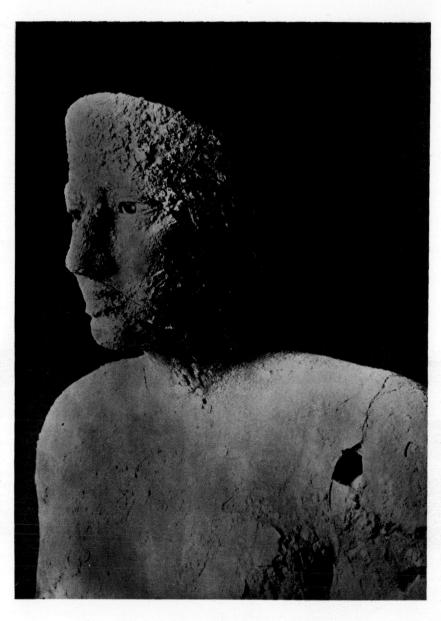

COPPER STATUES OF KING PEPI I AND HIS SON
DYNASTY VI   CAIRO MUSEUM

1. LIMESTONE STATUETTE OF A MAN KNEADING DOUGH
DYNASTY V   LOUVRE

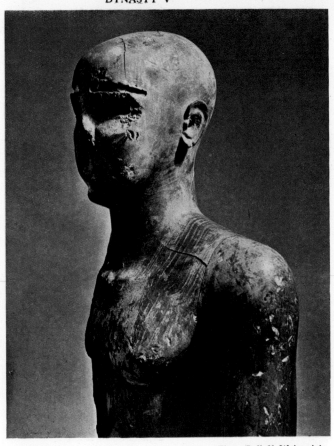

Photo. Dell & Wainwright

2. PART OF A WOODEN STATUE FROM ASSIUT
DYNASTY VI   BRITISH MUSEUM

3. LIMESTONE STATUE OF A DWARF, KHNEMHETEP
DYNASTY V   CAIRO MUSEUM

Photo, Dell & Wainwright

1. WOODEN PORTRAIT STATUE OF A GOVERNOR
DYNASTY VI   BRITISH MUSEUM

Photo, Dell & Wainwright

2. PAINTED LIMESTONE STATUE OF A ROYAL
KINSMAN. NEN-KHEFT-KA
DYNASTY V   BRITISH MUSEUM

Photo, Dell & Wainwright

2. PAINTED WOODEN PORTRAIT STATUE
DYNASTY VI   BRITISH MUSEUM

Photo, Dell & Wainwright

1. WOODEN PORTRAIT STATUE OF A CHANCELLOR,
THETI. DYNASTY VI   BRITISH MUSEUM

III

WOODEN STATUES OF AN EGYPTIAN OFFICIAL AND HIS WIFE
DYNASTY V   LOUVRE

WOODEN DOORS FROM THE TOMB OF
HESIRA' AT SAĶĶARA
DYNASTY IV   CAIRO MUSEUM
Photos, Exclusive News Agency

Photo, Deutscher Kunstverlag

1. LIMESTONE RELIEF OF DONKEYS FROM A TOMB
   DYNASTIES V-VI
   BERLIN

2. COLUMNS IN THE TOMB OF NEFERSESHEMRA' AT SAĶĶARA.   DYNASTY VI
   By courtesy of M. Jean Capart. From "Une Rue de Tombeaux à Saqqarah." Pl. xvi

3. LIMESTONE RELIEF OF DONKEYS FROM A MEMPHITE TOMB
   DYNASTIES V-VI .
   LEIDEN

LIMESTONE RELIEFS, DEPICTING AGRICULTURAL SCENES AND SHIPBUILDING
DYNASTY V   TOMB OF TY, SAKKARA

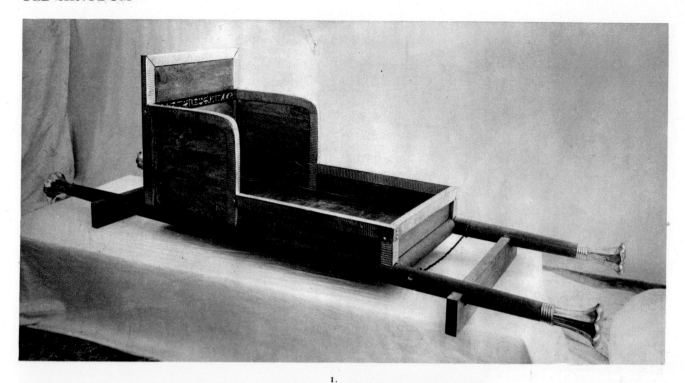

1.

2.

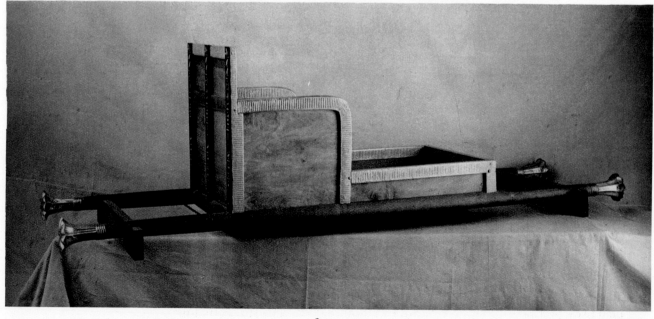

3.

HOUSEHOLD FURNITURE IN EBONY AND GOLD FROM THE TOMB OF QUEEN HETEP-HERES

1. and 3. The carrying-chair.
2. Detail of inscription, seen in Fig. 1., made by setting solid gold hieroglyphs in strips of ebony.
4. Back of the carrying-chair, seen in Fig. 3.
5. Armchair.

By courtesy of Professor Reisner

4.

5.

ALABASTER VASES
BRITISH MUSEUM

1. Dynasties III-IV.
2. Inscribed with the names of Isesi (Dynasty V) and Pepi I (Dynasty VI).
3. Inscribed with the name of Merenra' (Dynasty VI).

Photos, Dell & Wainwright

1. DIORITE VASES OF DYNASTIES III-V

2. RED POLISHED POTTERY BOWLS AND STANDS
DYNASTIES IV-VI

Steatite, enlarged 2½ times.

Blue frit, actual size.

Steatite, actual size.

Steatite, actual size.

STEATITE AND BLUE FRIT CYLINDER-SEALS, INSCRIBED WITH THE NAME OF PEPI I
DYNASTY VI   BRITISH MUSEUM

Photos, Dell & Wainwright

INTERMEDIATE PERIOD

SEVENTH DYNASTY
EIGHTH DYNASTY
NINTH DYNASTY
TENTH DYNASTY

2475—2160 B.C.

MIDDLE KINGDOM

ELEVENTH DYNASTY   2160—1995 B.C.
TWELFTH DYNASTY   1995—1790 B.C.
THIRTEENTH DYNASTY   1790—   B.C.

Photo, Studio Films

FAIENCE PLAQUE OF KING PEPI I
OLD KINGDOM, DYNASTY VI

GROUP OF STEATITE AND IVORY BUTTON-SEALS
LATE OLD KINGDOM AND INTERMEDIATE PERIOD

GLAZED STEATITE CYLINDER-SEAL OF SEBEKNEFERU
MIDDLE KINGDOM, DYNASTY XII   BRITISH MUSEUM

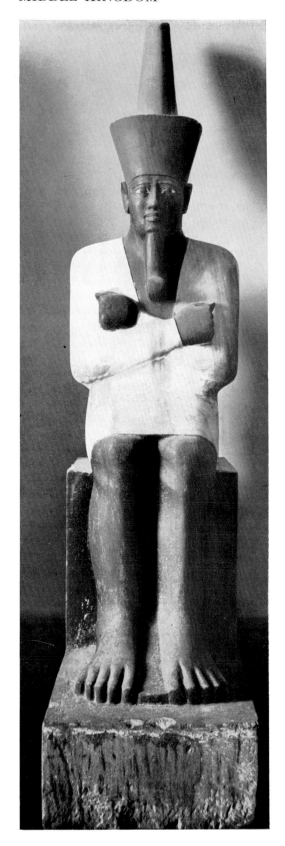

PAINTED SANDSTONE STATUE OF MENṬHOṬPE III
FROM HIS FUNERARY TEMPLE AT DÊR EL-BAḤRI
Height 6 ft.   CAIRO MUSEUM

*Reproduced from " Staat aus dem Stein," by Hans Evers, Verlag
F. Bruckman, A.-G., München. (Plate 12)*

ALABASTER STATUETTE OF MESEKHTI
FROM HIS TOMB AT ASYÛṬ
HERAKLEOPOLITAN PERIOD. Height 8¾ ins.   CAIRO MUSEUM

Reproduced from " Staat aus dem Stein," by Hans Evers, Verlag F. Bruckman, A.-G., München. (Plate 2)

BLACK GRANITE STATUE OF AMENEMḤET I
FOUND AT TANIS IN THE DELTA
Total height, 8 ft. 9½ ins.   CAIRO MUSEUM

Reproduced from " Staat aus dem Stein," by Hans Evers, Verlag F. Bruckman, A.-G., München. (Plate 17)

UPPER PART OF BLACK GRANITE STATUE OF SENUSRET I
FOUND AT ALEXANDRIA   Height of existing portion, 4 ft. 9¼ ins.   CAIRO MUSEUM

Reproduced from " Staat aus dem Stein," by Hans Evers, Verlag F. Bruckman, A.-G., München.   (Plate 36)

125

BLACK GRANITE STATUE OF NOFRET
WIFE OF SENUSRET I
FOUND AT TANIS. Height 3 ft. 8⅛ ins.   CAIRO MUSEUM

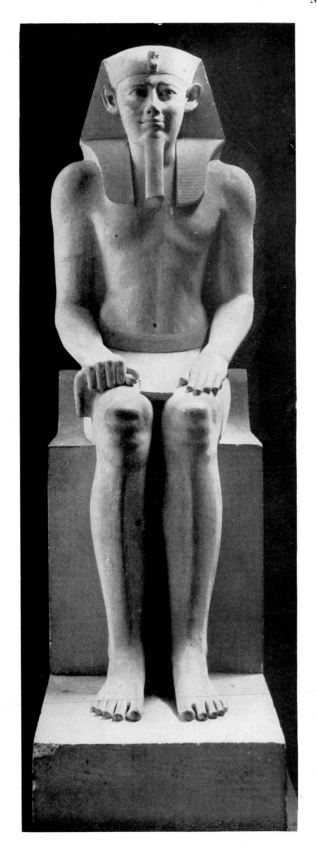

LIMESTONE STATUE
OF SENUSRET I
FROM HIS PYRAMID
TEMPLE AT LISHT
Height 6 ft. 6½ ins.
CAIRO MUSEUM

*Reproduced from " Staat aus
dem Stein " by Hans Evers.
Verlag F. Bruckman, A.-G.,
München. (Plate 27)*

Photo, Dell & Wainwright

BLACK GRANITE STATUE OF SENUSRET III
FROM DER EL-BAḤRI

Height, from top of head to just above knees, 4 ft. 11 ins.   BRITISH MUSEUM

By courtesy of Messrs. Spink & Son, Ltd.

HEAD OF AMENEMḤET III IN OBSIDIAN. Height, 4¼ ins.
IN THE COLLECTION OF M. C. S. GULBENKIAN

BLACK GRANITE HEAD OF SENUSRET III
FOUND AT MEDAMUT. Height, 11½ ins.   CAIRO MUSEUM

Reproduced from " Staat aus dem Stein," by Hans Evers, Verlag F. Bruckman, A.-G., München. (Plate 92)

UPPER PART OF BLACK GRANITE STATUE
OF AMENEMḤĒT III, FROM THE FAYYUM. Height 3 ft. 3⅜ ins.   CAIRO MUSEUM

Reproduced from " Staat aus dem Stein," by Hans Evers, Verlag F. Bruckman, A.-G., München. (Plate 127)

1. HEAD OF AMŪN WITH THE FEATURES OF AMENEM-ḤET III. Height, 7⅛ ins.
CAIRO MUSEUM

Reproduced from " Staat aus dem Stein," by Hans Evers, Verlag F. Bruckman, A.-G., München. (Fig. 26)

2. BLACK GRANITE SPHINX WITH THE HEAD OF AMEN-EMḤET III, FROM TANIS
Length, 7 ft. 4⅝ ins.
CAIRO MUSEUM

HEAD OF AMENEMḤET III, IN
GREEN SLATE. PROVENANCE
UNKNOWN. Height, 1 ft. 7 ins.
COPENHAGEN MUSEUM

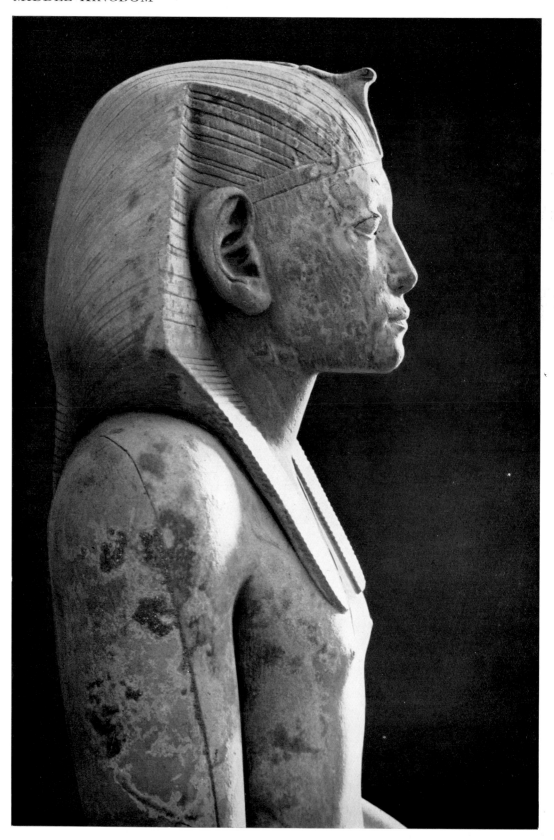

HEAD OF LIMESTONE STATUE OF AMENEMḤĒT III
FROM HIS PYRAMID-TEMPLE AT HAWARA   CAIRO MUSEUM
Total Height, 5 ft. 3 ins.

Reproduced from " Staat aus dem Stein," by Hans Evers, Verlag F. Bruckman, A.-G., München. (Plate 103)

Photo, Staatlichen Bildstelle, Berlin

1. DARK GREY GRANITE STATUE
OF THE LADY SENNUI
FROM KERMA IN THE SUDAN
Height, 5 ft. 6¼ ins.   BOSTON MUSEUM

2. BROWN CRYSTALLINE SANDSTONE STATUE
OF A SEATED MAN WRAPPED IN A CLOAK
FROM THE NEIGHBOURHOOD OF ASYÛṬ
Height, 2 ft. 5½ ins.   BERLIN MUSEUM

1

3

2

4

1. RED QUARTZITE STATUETTE OF PTAḤ-EM-SAF-SENEBTIFI
Height, 1 ft. 8½ ins.   BRITISH MUSEUM
Photo, Dell & Wainwright

2. BROWN SANDSTONE STATUETTE OF AMENEMḤET-'ONKH
Height, 2 ft. 4⅜ ins.   LOUVRE

3. SEATED LIMESTONE STATUE OF ANTEF, SON OF SEBEK-UNNU
Height, 2 ft. 1½ ins.   BRITISH MUSEUM
Photo, Dell & Wainwright

4. GREY GRANITE STATUE OF A NOBLE OF THE CITY OF ATHRIBIS, FROM BENHA, IN LOWER EGYPT
Height, 2 ft. 1 in.   BRITISH MUSEUM
Photo, Dell & Wainwright

Photo, Dell & Wainwright

Photo, Dell & Wainwright.

1. LIMESTONE STATUETTES OF MERI,
   AN OFFICIAL OF THE XIth DYNASTY
   FOUND AT KURNEH.
   Height, 8 ins. (nearer figure)   BRITISH MUSEUM

2. PAINTED WOODEN STATUETTE
   OF A WOMAN CARRYING
   A BASKET ON HER HEAD
   Height, 2 ft. 10 ins.   BRITISH MUSEUM

137

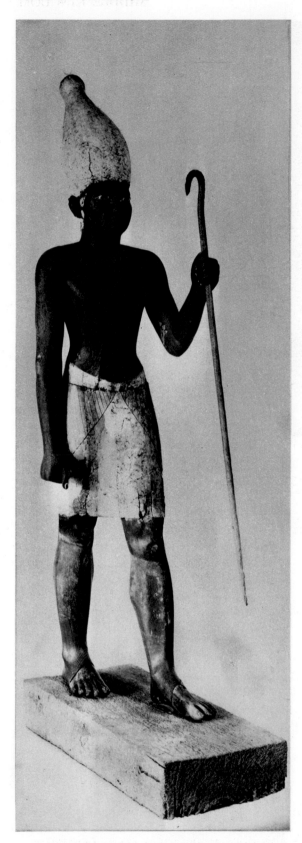

1. PAINTED WOODEN STATUETTE OF
SENUSRET I
FOUND IN A GRAVE CLOSE TO
HIS PYRAMID TEMPLE AT LISHT
Height, 1 ft. 10½ ins.   CAIRO MUSEUM

2. WOODEN STATUE OF THE "KA"
OF KING HORUS
FOUND IN HIS TOMB AT
DAHSHUR
Height, 5 ft. 9 ins.
                          CAIRO MUSEUM

1. HEAD OF A STATUE OF
A PRIVATE PERSONAGE
XIIth DYNASTY
Height, 8½ ins.
BRITISH MUSEUM

2. PAINTED EBONY STATUETTE OF THE
HERAKLEOPOLITAN PERIOD
Height, 2 ft. 3⅛ ins.
COLLECTION OF M. C. S. GULBENKIAN

3. WOODEN MODEL OF A COOK FANNING A
BRAZIER OVER WHICH HE IS ROASTING
A GOOSE (broken off) ON A SPIT
PROBABLY OF THE HERAKLEOPOLITAN
PERIOD   BRITISH MUSEUM

WOODEN MODELS.

1. A sailing boat with its crew from Beni Hasan.
   Herakleopolitan period.
   Ashmolean Museum, Oxford.
   Photo, Dell & Wainwright

2. Meketre seated in a portico, inspecting cattle driven past him by herdsmen.
   From the tomb of Meketre, Thebes.
   XIth dynasty.   Cairo Museum.

3. Heavy-armed infantry.
   Found in the tomb of Mesekhti at Asyut.
                    Cairo Museum.

1. FISHERMEN FISHING
WITH A DRAG NET
WOODEN MODEL FOUND
IN THE TOMB OF
MEKETRE AT THEBES
CAIRO MUSEUM

2. WOODEN MODEL OF
PEASANTS PLOUGHING
WITH A YOKE OF OXEN
PROBABLY HERACLEO-
POLITAN PERIOD
BRITISH MUSEUM
Photo, Dell & Wainwright

3. THREE OF THE FOUR
CANOPIC JARS OF
GUA-TEP WITH THE
CHEST TO CONTAIN
THEM   BRITISH MUSEUM
Photo, Dell & Wainwright

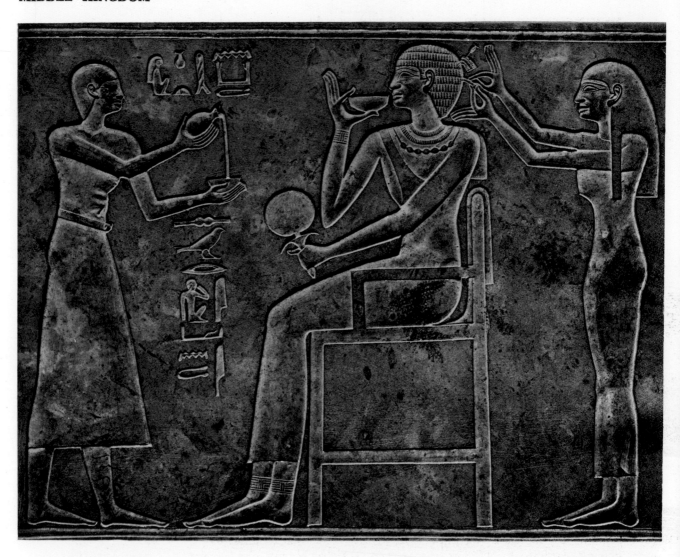

1. THE PRINCESS KAWIT TAKING REFRESHMENT WHILE HER HAIR
   IS BEING DRESSED
   ONE OF THE RELIEFS ADORNING HER LIMESTONE SARCOPHAGUS
   FOUND AT DER EL-BAHRI   CAIRO MUSEUM

2. PAINTED RELIEF DEPICTING THE ARMED BODY-GUARD AND CHAIRMEN OF DJHUTHOTPE,
   HIS DOG, ANKHU BY NAME, WALKS BENEATH HIS MASTER'S CHAIR
   FROM HIS TOMB AT EL-BERSHEH
   PROBABLY DATING FROM THE REIGN OF SENUSRET III   BRITISH MUSEUM

142

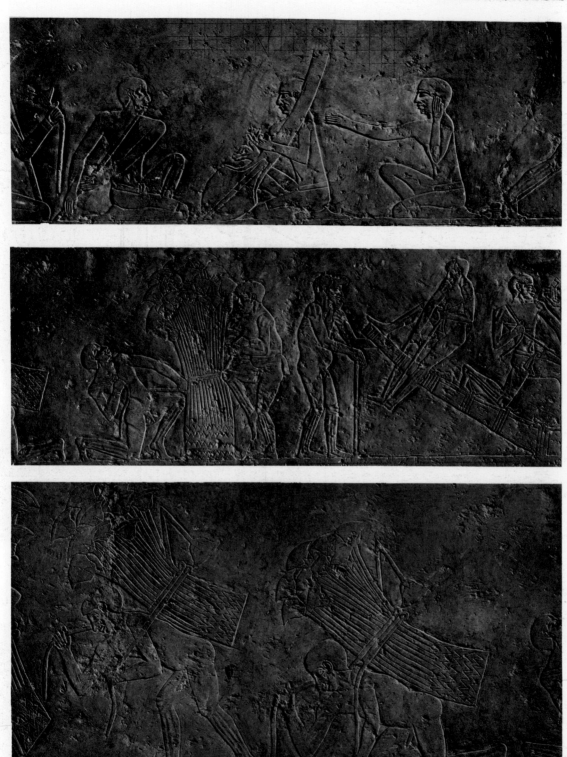

RELIEFS FROM THE TOMB-CHAPEL OF UKH-ḤOTPE, SON OF SENBI, AT MER
EARLY XIIth DYNASTY

1. A flautist and a blind singer and harpist.
2. Two peasants binding a bundle of papyrus reeds, and a fat old man conversing with a ship-builder.
3. Two papyrus harvesters.   (See Blackman, " The Rock Tombs of Meir.")

1. A BISHARI HERDSMAN WITH SOME OF HIS CATTLE
RELIEF FROM THE TOMB OF UKH-ḤOTPE AT MER
EARLY XIIth DYNASTY

2. INNER SIDE OF AN ELABORATELY PAINTED WOODEN SARCOPHAGUS
HERACLEOPOLITAN PERIOD. FOUND AT BERSHEH

CAIRO MUSEUM

1. WALL-PAINTING IN THE TOMB-CHAPEL OF ANTEFOḲER AT THEBES
DEPICTING A NUMBER OF DANCING GIRLS
From Davies, " The Tomb of Antefoḳer" (Plate xxiii A).

2. WALL-PAINTING IN THE TOMB-CHAPEL OF ḴHNEMḤOTPE
TWO FARM HANDS ATTENDING A COUPLE OF ORYXES
From Newberry, " Beni Hasan" I (Plate xvii).

TWO CORONETS OF PRINCESS KHNEMIT FROM DAHSHUR   CAIRO MUSEUM

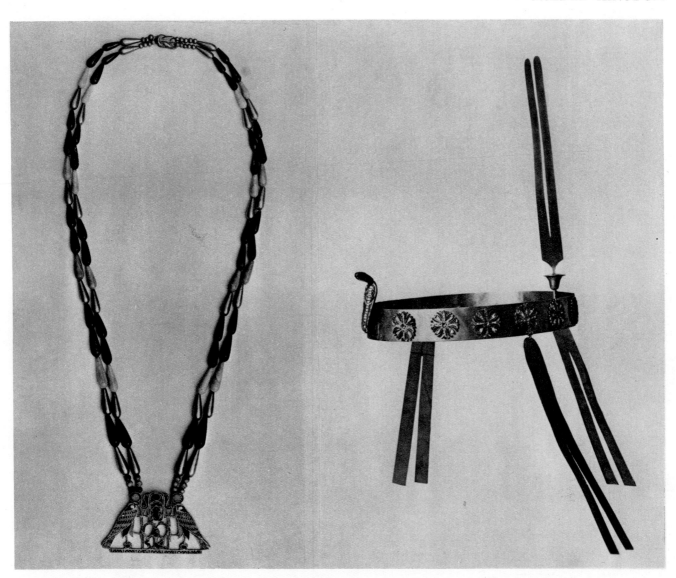

1. PECTORAL OF
   SENUSRET II
   ON A NECKLACE
   OF SEMI-PRECIOUS
   STONES
   METROPOLITAN
   MUSEUM OF ART,
   NEW YORK

2. GOLD CROWN OF PRINCESS
   SAT-ḤATHOR-IUNUT
   FROM HER TOMB NEAR THE
   PYRAMID OF SENUSRET II
   ILLAHUN
   XIIth DYNASTY
       CAIRO MUSEUM

3. PECTORAL OF
   AMENEMḤET III
   CAIRO MUSEUM

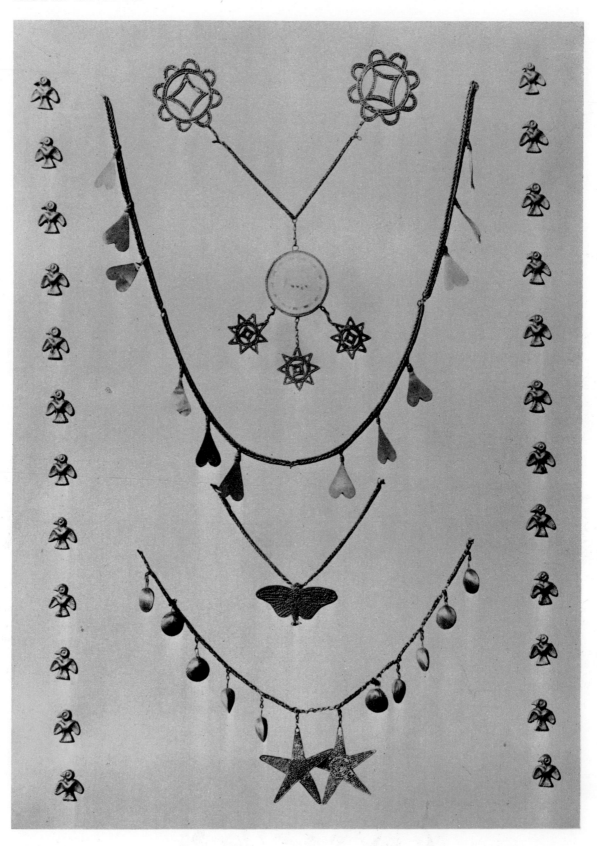

JEWELLERY FROM DAHSHUR   CAIRO MUSEUM

ALABASTER AND OBSIDIAN
TOILET VASES

METROPOLITAN MUSEUM OF ART
NEW YORK

1. GROUP OF SMALL GLAZE FIGURES

Photo, Studio Films
BRITISH MUSEUM

An ape with a kohl-pot, an hedgehog, a dwarf, a musician, a dwarf, a puppy, a musician and a mouse.

Photo, Studio Films

2. FOUR BUTTON SEALS (See also p. 121).

BRITISH MUSEUM

1. GLAZE HIPPOPOTAMUS
AND PUPPY
BRITISH MUSEUM.
Photo, Dell & Wainwright

2. WHITE GLAZE MOUSE
COLLECTION OF
A. M. BLACKMAN, ESQ.
Photo, Dell & Wainwright

1. EXTERIOR OF THE TOMB OF
KHNEMHOTPE AT BENI HASAN
From Jean Capart, " L'Art égyptien"
(Plate 68).

2. RESTORATION OF THE TEMPLE
OF MENTHOTPE III.
From Naville, " The XIth Dynasty Temple
of Der el-Bahri."

3. [NEW KINGDOM]

EXTERIOR OF THE CHAPEL OF
ANUBIS AT DER EL-BAHRI
From Borchardt & Ricke, " Egypt" (Orbis
Terrarum).

HYKSOS DYNASTIES

FOURTEENTH—
SEVENTEENTH DYNASTIES   —1580 B.C.

NEW KINGDOM

EIGHTEENTH DYNASTY   1580—1350 B.C.
NINETEENTH DYNASTY   1350—1200 B.C.
TWENTIETH DYNASTY   1200—1090 B.C.
TWENTY-FIRST DYNASTY   1090 — 945 B.C.
TWENTY-SECOND—
TWENTY-FOURTH DYNASTIES   945 — 712 B.C.

VIEW OF THE COLUMNED HALL OF AMENHOTEP III's TEMPLE AT LUXOR

1. A COLOSSAL STATUE OF RAMSES II WITH HIS QUEEN
   BESIDE HIM   LUXOR

2. QUEEN NEFRETARI AT THE SIDE OF THE COLOSSAL
   STATUE OF RAMSES II   LUXOR

THE HYPOSTYLE HALL OF SETI I   AT KARNAK

VIEW OF THE MORTUARY TEMPLE OF HATSHEPSUT. DER EL BAHARI

THE HATHOR COW FROM DER EL BAHARI   CAIRO MUSEUM

SCULPTURE IN RELIEF : FROM HATSHEPSUT'S TEMPLE AT DER EL BAHARI

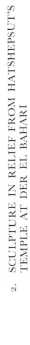

2. SCULPTURE IN RELIEF FROM HATSHEPSUT'S
TEMPLE AT DER EL BAHARI

1. SCULPTURE IN RELIEF *EN CREUX* FROM
HATSHEPSUT'S TEMPLE AT DER EL BAHARI

1. A BANQUET SCENE FROM A TOMB AT THEBES   BRITISH MUSEUM

2. A FOWLING SCENE FROM
   A TOMB AT THEBES   BRITISH MUSEUM

FRONT VIEW OF THE BODY OF THE CHARIOT OF THUTMOSE IV   CAIRO MUSEUM

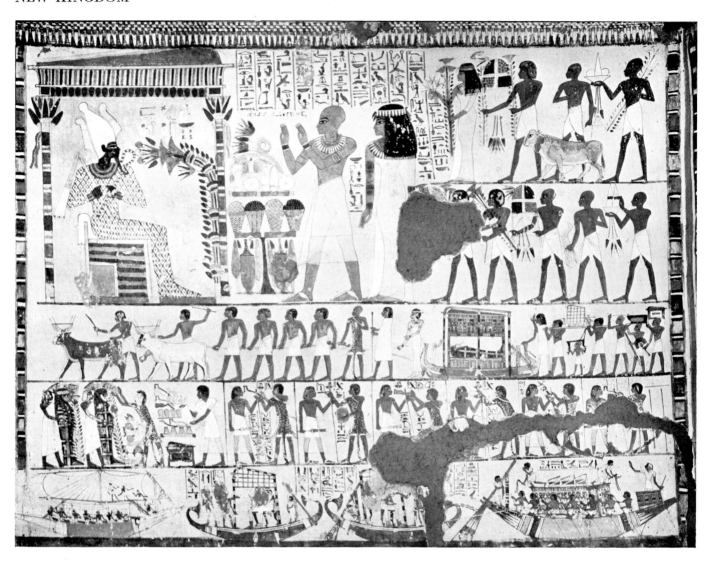

A TYPICAL TOMB-PAINTING OF THE TIME OF
AMENHOTEP III DRAWN ACCORDING TO THE
TRADITIONAL CANONS OF ART   THEBES

AN ARTIST'S STUDY OF ONE OF THE PRINCESSES SEATED ON A
CUSHION AND EATING A BIRD   CAIRO MUSEUM

A SLAB SCULPTURED IN RELIEF *EN CREUX* DEPICTING IKHNATON
OFFERING TO THE ATEN   CAIRO MUSEUM

A SLAB SCULPTURED IN RELIEF *EN CREUX*
DEPICTING IKHNATON WITH HIS FAMILY
BERLIN MUSEUM

1. PAINTED SCENE OF HOREMHEB AS KING OFFERING TO THE GODS FROM HIS TOMB AT THEBES

2. A SLAB SCULPTURED IN RELIEF *EN CREUX* FROM THE MEMPHITE TOMB OF HOREMHEB
LEYDEN MUSEUM

VIEW OF THE INTERIOR OF A RAMESSIDE OFFICIAL'S TOMB AT THEBES

1. BAS-RELIEF FROM ABYDOS WITH SCENE DEPICTING RAMSES I AND SETI I OFFERING TO THE
CULT-OBJECT OF OSIRIS   METROPOLITAN MUSEUM OF ART, NEW YORK

2. FIGURES SCULPTURED IN RELIEF   THEBES
FROM THE TOMB OF RAMOSE

PIECE OF A TAPESTRY-WOVEN CORSELET OF AMENHOTEP II   CAIRO MUSEUM

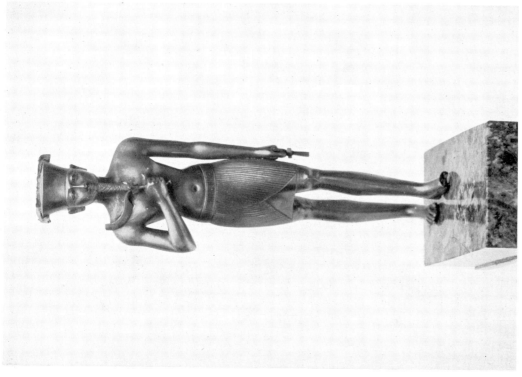

2. GOLD STATUETTE OF THE GOD AMON   METROPOLITAN
IN THE LIKENESS OF THUTMOSE III.   MUS., NEW YORK

Photo, Dell & Wainwright

BRITISH MUSEUM

1. LIMESTONE STATUETTE
OF TETISHERI

UPPER PART OF BASALT STATUE OF THUTMOSE III   CAIRO MUSEUM

1. COLOSSAL FIGURE OF IKHNATON FROM
HIS TEMPLE AT KARNAK   CAIRO

2. STATUETTE OF QUEEN ISIS   CAIRO
MOTHER OF THUTMOSE III   MUSEUM

GROUP OF A MAYOR OF THEBES
WITH HIS WIFE AND DAUGHTER   CAIRO MUSEUM

THE SCRIBE AMENHOTEP SON OF HAPU   CAIRO MUSEUM

THE SCRIBE HOREMHEB   METROPOLITAN MUSEUM OF ART, NEW YORK

1. MODEL HEADS IN PLASTER FROM THE SCULPTOR'S STUDIO AT EL AMARNA   BERLIN MUSEUM

2. MODEL HEAD IN PLASTER OF AMENHOTEP III FROM EL AMARNA   BERLIN MUSEUM

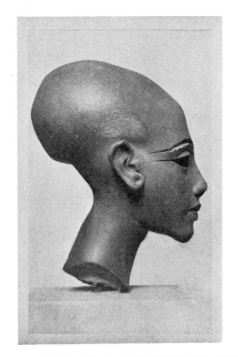

1. HEAD OF A DAUGHTER OF IKHNATON IN FINE-GRAINED CRYSTALLINE
SANDSTONE   BERLIN MUSEUM

2. HEAD OF NEFRETITI IN FINE-GRAINED CRYSTALLINE SANDSTONE
                                                       BERLIN MUSEUM

(a) Fragment of a head in calcareous limestone.

(b) Fragment of a head in yellow jasper.

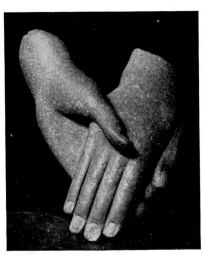

(c) Two hands from a statue group.

1. THREE FRAGMENTS OF SCULPTURE
   FROM EL AMARNA

(a) and (b) are in the Metropolitan Museum of Art
(c) is at Berlin.

2. TORSO OF A STATUETTE OF ONE OF THE
   ROYAL PRINCESSES FROM EL AMARNA
   UNIVERSITY COLLEGE, LONDON

Photo, Studio Films

1. STATUETTES IN WOOD OF THE   CAIRO
    LATE XVIIITH AND XIXTH DYNASTIES   MUSEUM

Photo, Dell & Wainwright

2. TOILET OR PERFUME LADLE IN WOOD OF THE XVIIITH OR XIXTH DYNASTY   BRITISH MUSEUM

TOILET OR PERFUME LADLE IN WOOD
OF THE XVIIITH OR XIXTH DYNASTY   LOUVRE

CHAIR OF AMENHOTEP III's ELDEST
DAUGHTER SATAMEN

CAIRO MUSEUM

JEWEL CASE OF AMENHOTEP III IN WOOD
INLAID WITH POLYCHROME FAIENCE

CAIRO MUSEUM

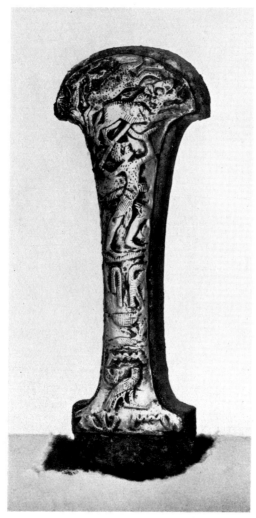

1. ENGRAVED HILT OF THE
   DAGGER OF A HYKSOS KING
   CAIRO MUSEUM

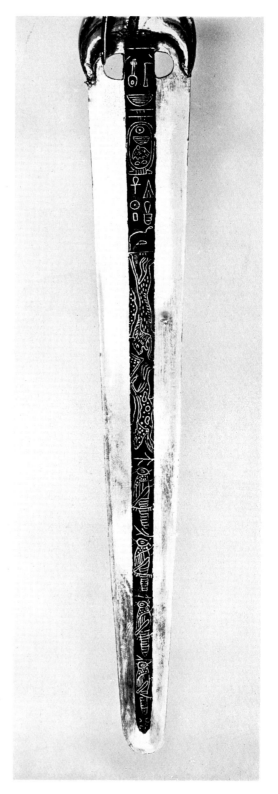

2. ENGRAVED BLADE OF THE
   DAGGER OF AHMOSE I
   CAIRO MUSEUM

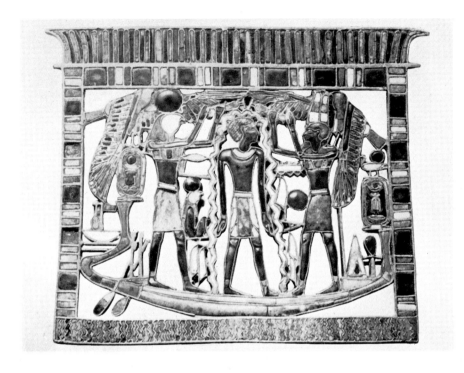

1. PECTORAL OF
AHMOSE I
CAIRO MUSEUM

2. ARMLET FROM
THE TOMB OF
QUEEN ANHOTEP
CAIRO MUSEUM

185

Above : GOLD BRACELET WITH THE NAME OF RAMESES II
Below : SILVER BRACELET OF QUEEN TAUOSRIT   CAIRO MUSEUM

WALL-TILES IN POLYCHROME FAIENCE FROM THE PALACE OF RAMSES III   BERLIN MUSEUM

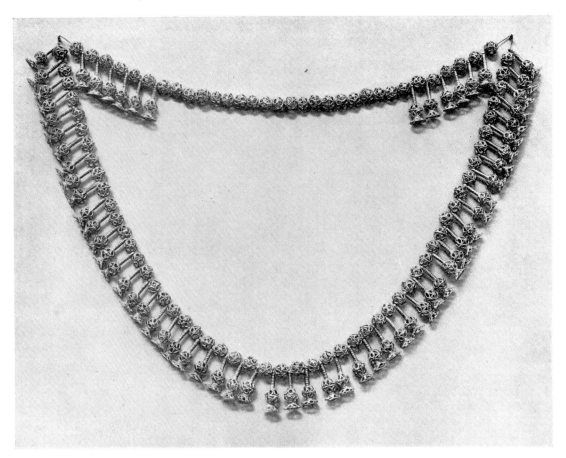

1. GOLD NECKLACE OF QUEEN TAUOSRIT   CAIRO MUSEUM

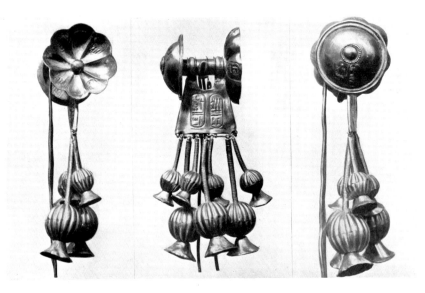

2. CEREMONIAL WIG-ORNAMENTS OF SETI II CAIRO MUSEUM

1. BLUE GLAZED FAIENCE BOWL OF
THE EARLY XVIIIth DYNASTY   LOUVRE

2. CHALICE IN BLUE   MYERS COLL.
GLAZED FAIENCE. ETON COLLEGE

3. CHALICE IN   METROPOLITAN MUSEUM
BLUE GLAZED FAIENCE. OF ART, NEW YORK

4. CHALICE IN GLASS WITH THE NAME
OF THUTMOSE III INLAID. MUNICH

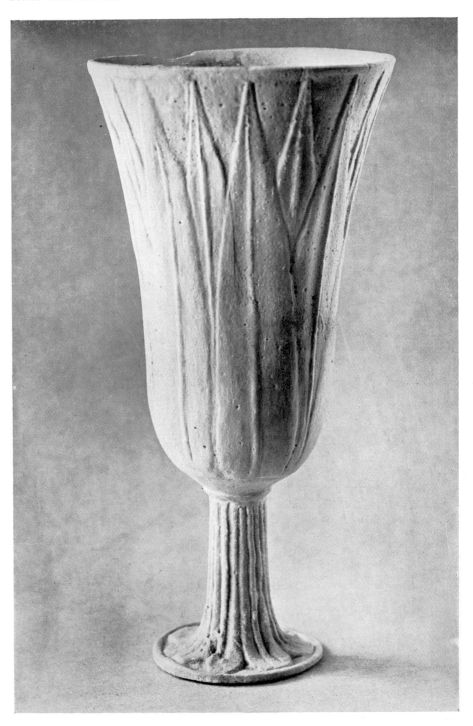

FAIENCE LOTUS VASE   ASHMOLEAN MUSEUM, OXFORD

TUTANKHAMEN

THE OUTERMOST OF THE THREE COFFINS ENCLOSING THE MUMMY OF TUTANKHAMEN

(See Page 203)

BACK PANEL OF THE THRONE OF TUTANKHAMEN

The scene depicts the king and his queen Ankh-es-en-Amen. It is overlaid with sheet-gold and richly inlaid with coloured
faience, glass and semi-precious stones (see page 211).

TUTANKHAMEN AND HIS QUEEN SHOOTING WILD FOWL

From one of the embossed gold panels upon a miniature shrine.

TUTANKHAMEN AND HIS WIFE ANKH-ES-EN-AMEN IN A PAVILION
BEDECKED WITH FESTOONS OF FLOWERS

The scene forms the central panel upon the lid of a casket. It is carved in low bas-relief
on ivory and stained. In the frieze below are court maidens gathering flowers and the
fruit of the mandragor.

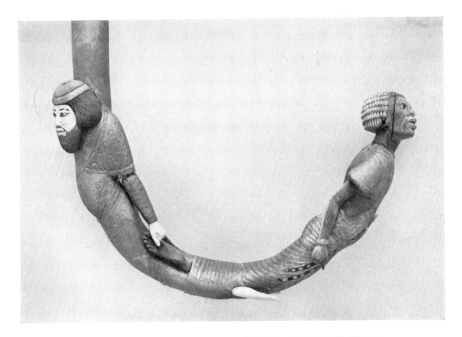

THE HANDLE OF A CEREMONIAL WALKING-STICK

Bound to the handle of this stick are two prisoners, symbolizing the Northern and Southern foes of Egypt. The Asiatic type is carved of ivory, the African type of ebony. Their dresses are of argentiferous gold embellished with inlay.

TWO VIEWS OF THE KING'S GOLD STICK

A BATTLE SCENE IN MINIATURE PAINTING

From a painted casket. 1. The king is here represented slaughtering the Asiatic enemies of Egypt. The whole mass of this ornament is made up of multitudinous human figures in every kind of action—and magnificent action. The king is shown in his chariot, drawing his bow, his sheaves of arrows rattling at his sides, and the slain falling under him as before a pestilence. 2. Detail of the Asiatic enemies.

196

A HUNTING SCENE IN MINIATURE PAINTING

From a painted casket. 1. In the centre we see the king in his chariot hunting lions and lionesses. Behind the
king are represented his fan-bearers, courtiers and bodyguard.   In the field are depicted desert flora. 2. Details
of the lions and lionesses.

TUTANKHAMEN AS THE YOUTHFUL WARRIOR HORUS

This statuette represents the king throwing a javelin at the typhonial animal hiding in the marsh. It is carved of a hard wood and overlaid with thin sheet-gold. The reed float is painted green.

TUTANKHAMEN UPON A BLACK LEOPARD

The king is here represented wearing the White Crown of Upper Egypt, the long *Shendyt*-kilt, sandals, and in his hands he holds the straight-staff of seniority and the flagellum. The meaning of this statuette is not understood: it is carved of a hard wood, the king overlaid with thin sheet-gold, the leopard painted with a black resin.

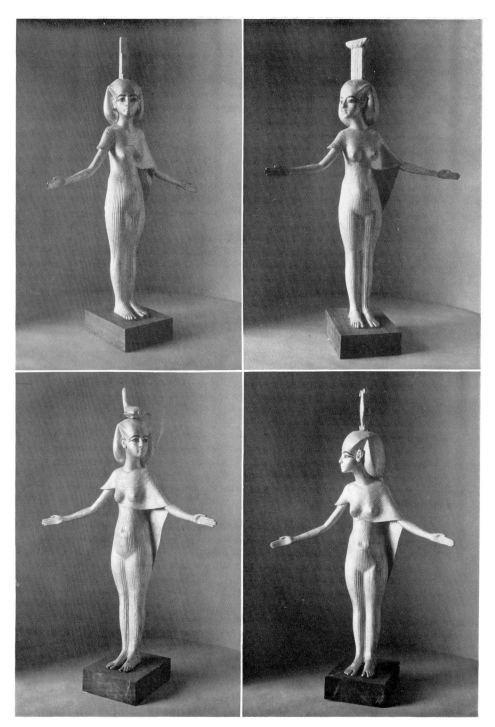

FOUR GODDESSES

These four tutelary goddesses, (1) ISIS, (2) NEPHTHYS, (3) SELKIT, and (4) NEITH,
protected Tutankhamen's Canopic equipment. They are about two feet in height, are
carved of a hard wood and are overlaid with thin sheet-gold.

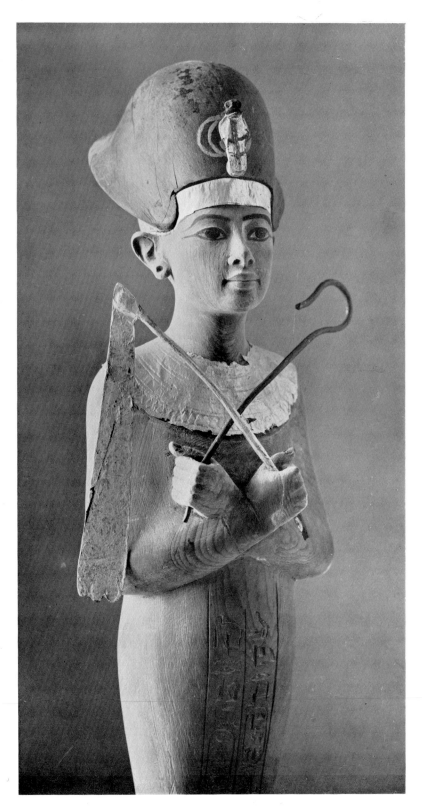

A SHAWABTI-FIGURE OF
TUTANKHAMEN

It is carved of a coniferous wood, the
emblems and collar gilt, the headdress
of ebony.

TWO LIFE-SIZE STATUES OF TUTANKHAMEN

These statues are of wood, covered with a black resin, the headdress, collar, dress, sandals, sceptres and staves gilt.

TWO OF THE THREE COFFINS THAT ENCLOSED THE MUMMY OF TUTANKHAMEN

The first, the outermost, coffin (see p. 191) is carved of an oaken wood and overlaid with sheet-gold. The insignia upon the forehead and the emblems in the hands are inlaid with opaque coloured glass and faience (p. 191). The second coffin (right), carved of an oaken wood and overlaid with sheet-gold, is sumptuously inlaid with opaque coloured glass simulating red jasper, lapis lazuli and turquoise respectively. The innermost coffin (left) is wrought of solid gold, elaborately chased, and embellished with superimposed *cloisonné* work.

TUTANKHAMEN'S GOLD MASK

A beaten and burnished gold mask representing the king at the age of death—about 18 years of age. The head-dress and collar are inlaid with opaque polychrome glass imitating semi-precious stones.

TWO RIGID PECTORAL ORNAMENTS

Inlaid with semi-precious stones and coloured glass.

SPECIMENS OF JEWELLERY

(1) *Cloisonné* work ear-rings. The heads of the birds are of translucent dark blue glass. (2) Ear-rings of yellow granulated gold-work upon scarlet gold, intermixed with resin beads. (3 and 4) Pectoral ornaments of gold and silver worked *à jour* and inlaid with various semi-precious stones and coloured glass. (5) A Flexible Pectoral Ornament, comprising a pectoral ornament, suspension straps and clasp, composed of many parts strung together with various kinds of beads.

1. A LOTIFORM CALCITE WISHING-CUP

2. A CALCITE TRIPLE-LAMP OR TRICERION OF LOTIFORM

207

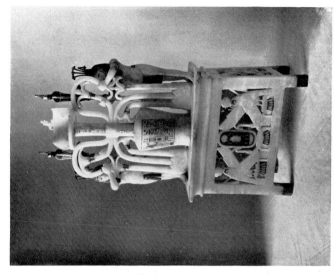

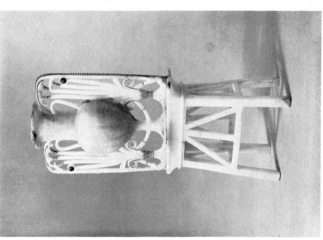

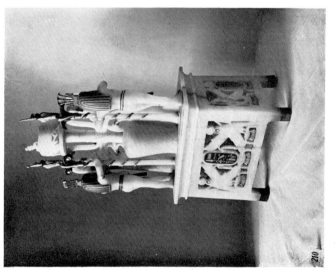

(RIGHT AND LEFT) TWO VIEWS OF AN INTRICATE CALCITE UNGUENT VASE

(CENTRE) A CALCITE UNGUENT VASE WITH FLANKING ORNAMENT

(2) A CALCITE COSMETIC JAR

The tongue of the lion, the hinge of the lid and the knobs are of ivory stained red. The heads of the prisoners forming the feet are of red and black stone.

(1) A CALCITE UNGUENT VASE IN THE FORM OF A HERALDIC LION

The tongue and teeth are of ivory. The design symbolizes " protection."

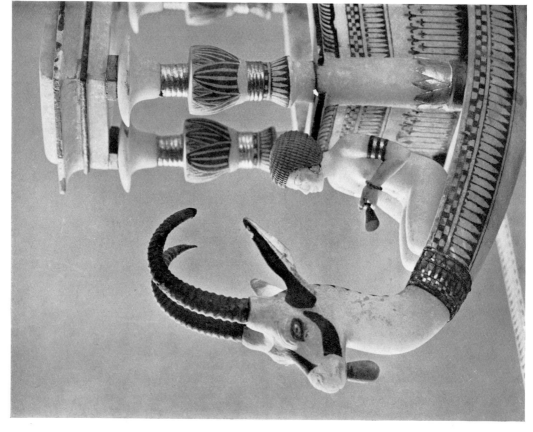

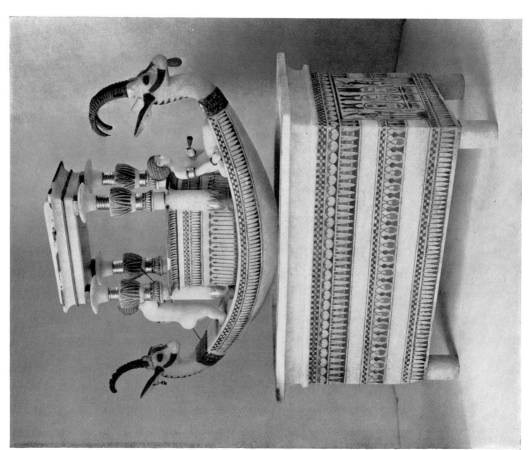

A CALCITE CENTRE-PIECE

In the form of an ornamental boat in a tank. The details are incised and filled in with pigment, the embellishments are of gold. Right: Details of the figure on the foredeck and ibex head.

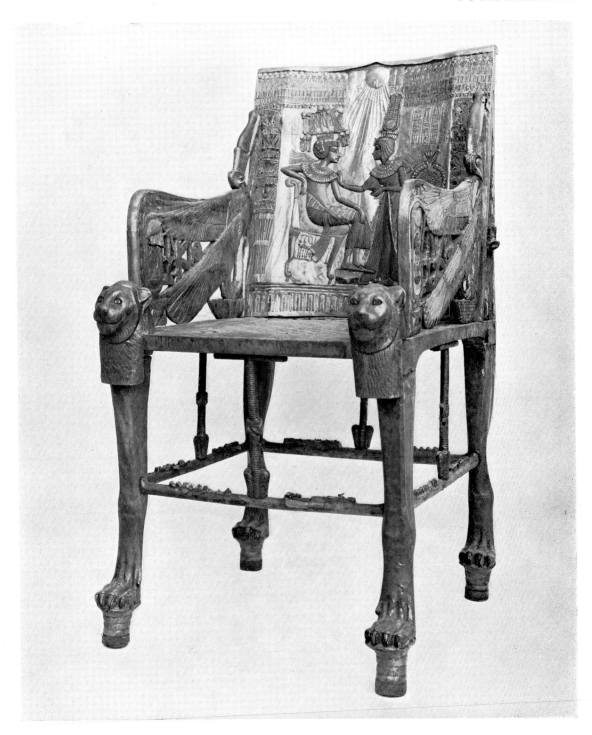

THE KING'S GOLDEN THRONE

Carved of wood, overlaid with sheet-gold, and richly inlaid with coloured glass, faience and semi-precious stones. (see p. 192)

A CARVED CEDAR-WOOD CHAIR

The embellishments are of gold.

1. A CHILD'S STOOL
Made of cedar-wood inlaid with ebony and ivory.

2. A CHILD'S CHAIR
Carved of ebony and inlaid with ivory.

A CASKET UPON A STAND

The framework is of ebony, the panels of cedar-wood, and between the casket and stretchers a
fretwork of alternate gilt and plain ebony symbols meaning " All life and wealth."

A CEDAR-WOOD CASKET

The casket, inlaid with ebony and ivory, is carried on poles sliding in staples fixed on the bottom.

A BOW CASE

Ornamented with marquetry of variegated barks, applied strips of tinted leather, gold foil, and iridescent beetles' wings.
Above, detail of one of the panels.

1. AN ORNAMENTAL JEWEL BOX

Veneered with ivory and having panels decorated with minute marquetry inlay of ebony and ivory.

2. A CASKET FOR SIXTEEN VESSELS

Veneered with ivory, having panels of gilt fretwork symbols meaning "All life and wealth."

1. AN IVORY BOX FOR FINGER-RINGS

The knobs, hinges and feet casings are of gold.

2. A CARVED IVORY HEAD-REST

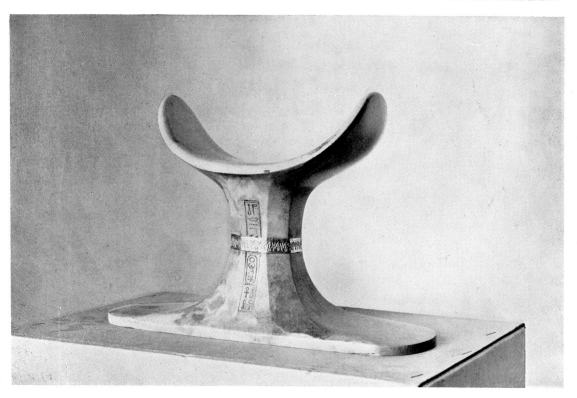

TWO HEAD-RESTS

(Above) Turquoise blue glass with gold collar round stem.
(Below) Lapis lazuli blue faience (glazed pottery), inlaid with light blue glaze, having an inlaid gold collar round stem.

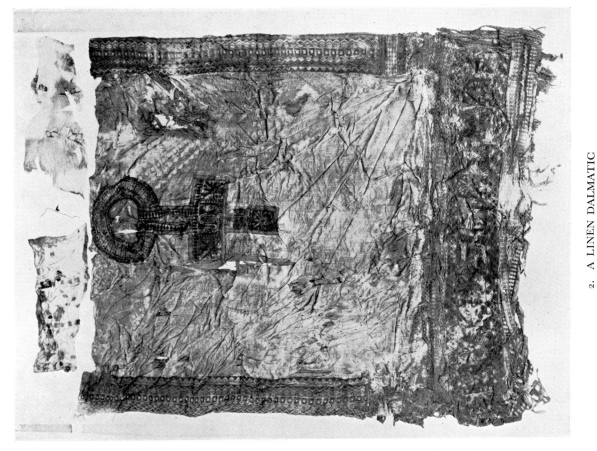

2. A LINEN DALMATIC

Ornamented with tapestry-woven decoration and needlework on broad hem at the bottom.

1. A GLOVE

Tapestry-woven linen.

SAÏTE PERIOD

TWENTY-FIFTH DYNASTY	712—663 B.C.
TWENTY-SIXTH DYNASTY	663—525 B.C.
TWENTY-SEVENTH DYNASTY	525—332 B.C.

PTOLEMAIC PERIOD
332-30 B.C.

ROMAN PERIOD
30 B.C.—395 A.D.

Photo, Beato

PAVILION AT PHILÆ
ROMAN PERIOD

TEMPLE OF HATHOR AT DENDERAH   *Photo, Ricke*
PTOLEMAIC PERIOD

TEMPLE OF HORUS AT EDFU   *Photo, Ricke*
SAITE PERIOD

DOUBLE COURT AND PRONAOS AT KOM OMBO
ROMAN PERIOD

TEMPLE OF HATHOR AT DENDERAH
PTOLEMAIC PERIOD

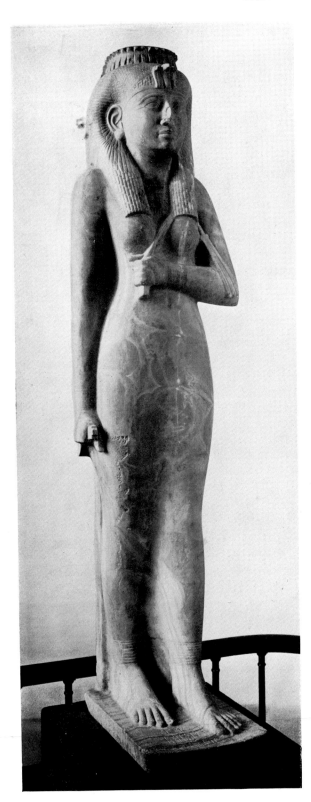

ALABASTER STATUE OF
QUEEN AMENARTAS
DYNASTY XXV
CAIRO MUSEUM

1. HEAD OF KING TIRHAKA
DYNASTY XXV (ETHIOPIAN)

CAIRO
MUSEUM

2. HEAD OF MENTUEMHAT
DYNASTY XXV (THEBAN)

CAIRO
MUSEUM

Photo, Dell & Wainwright

QUARTZITE HEAD OF AN OLD MAN
DYNASTY XXV (THEBAN)

BRITISH MUSEUM

227

RELIEF FROM THE TOMB OF ZANEFER AT MEMPHIS
DYNASTY XXVI

GRÆCO-ROMAN MUSEUM
ALEXANDRIA

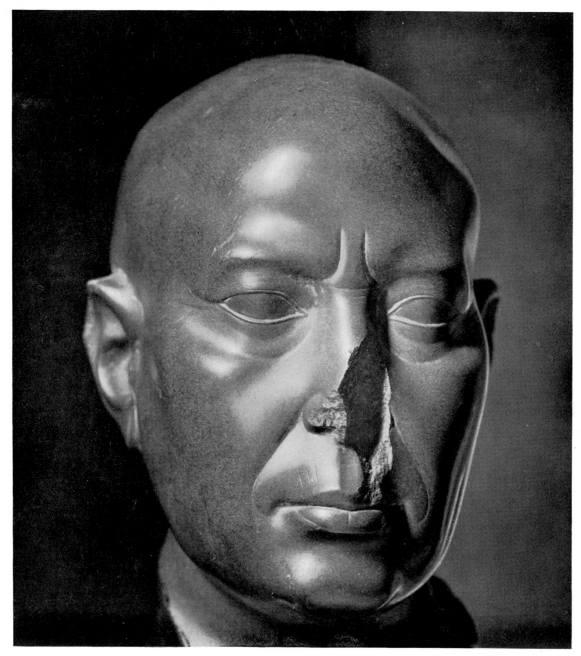

GREEN BASALT HEAD OF AN OLD MAN
FROM MEMPHIS
SAÏTE PERIOD   BERLIN MUSEUM

Photo, Staatliche Bildstelle, Berlin

BLACK GRANITE HEAD OF A YOUNG MAN
SAÏTE PERIOD

BERLIN MUSEUM

1. THREE VIEWS OF A BRONZE STATUE OF
TAKUSHET, INLAID WITH SILVER
DYNASTY XXV   ATHENS MUSEUM

2. BRONZE STATUE OF QUEEN KAROMAMA
ENCRUSTED WITH GOLD
DYNASTY XXV   LOUVRE

3. HATHOR COW OF PSAMMETICHUS
DYNASTY XXV   CAIRO

RELIEF OF NECTANEBO

DYNASTY XXX

BRITISH MUSEUM

GILT WOODEN COFFIN WITH INLAID EYES
PTOLEMAIC PERIOD   BERLIN MUSEUM

Photo, Dell & Wainwright

UPPER PART OF A BASALT STATUE
OF PTOLEMY AULETES
PTOLEMAIC PERIOD   BRITISH MUSEUM

1. RELIEF FROM THE TEMPLE AT KOM OMBO   *Photo, Dittrich*
PTOLEMY AMONG EGYPTIAN GODS

2. RELIEF FROM THE TOMB OF PET-OSIRIS

CLEOPATRA
RELIEF FROM
DENDERAH
PTOLEMAIC
PERIOD

Photo, Alinari

HEAD OF JULIUS CÆSAR
ROMAN PERIOD

MUSEO BARRACCO
ROME

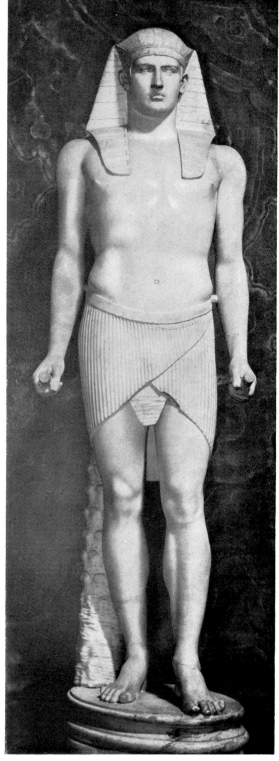

1. THE ALEXANDRIAN PRIEST HORUS
PTOLEMAIC PERIOD
CAIRO MUSEUM

2. STATUE OF ANTINOUS AS APOLLO
ROMAN PERIOD
FOUND AT HADRIAN'S VILLA
VATICAN MUSEUM

Photo, Alinari

Photo, Dell & Wainwright

HEAD OF SARAPIS
PTOLEMAIC PERIOD

BRITISH MUSEUM

1. STATUETTE OF HORUS AS A ROMAN GENERAL
   ROMAN PERIOD   BRITISH MUSEUM

2. STATUETTE OF AN OLD MAN
   ROMAN PERIOD   BRITISH MUSEUM

Photos, Dell & Wainwright

1. LIMESTONE FIGURE OF A DOG   LOUVRE
2. BRONZE FIGURE OF A CAT. SAITE PERIOD   LOUVRE
3. LID OF A BOX FROM THE TEMPLE OF ÆSCULAPIUS (*Photo, Exclusive News Agency*) CAIRO MUSEUM
4 and 5. STATUETTE OF A WOMAN. PTOLEMAIC PERIOD   ALEXANDRIA

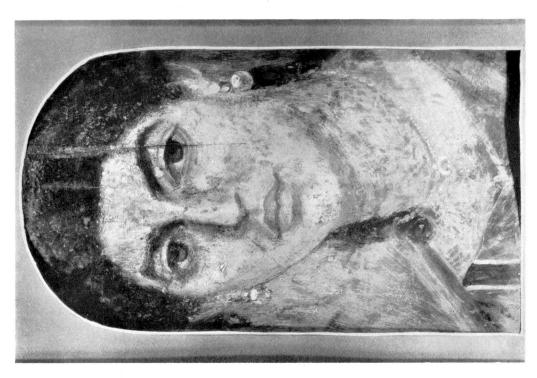

TWO PORTRAITS FROM FAYUM
ROMAN PERIOD

NATIONAL GALLERY
LONDON

PORTRAIT OF A YOUNG WOMAN
FROM FAYUM
1st—IIIrd CENTURY A.D.

NATIONAL GALLERY
MOND BEQUEST

Photo, Dell & Wainwright

PLASTER MASK FROM FAYUM
ROMAN PERIOD

UNIVERSITY COLLEGE
LONDON

1 *Photo, Dell & Wainwright*

4

2 *Photo, Dell & Wainwright* 3 *Photo, Dell & Wainwright*

1 and 2. FAIENCE BOWL AND RHYTON. DYNASTY XXVI BRITISH MUSEUM
3. FAIENCE HEAD OF ARSINOE II. PTOLEMAIC PERIOD BRITISH MUSEUM
4. FAIENCE DISH. ROMAN PERIOD VICTORIA AND ALBERT MUSEUM

COPTIC PERIOD

395—640 A.D.

HORUS AS A ROMAN HORSEMAN
PIERCING THE CROCODILE
FROM BAOUIT

LOUVRE

CHRISTIAN TOMB MONUMENTS IN THE KHARGA OASIS

Photos, Ricke

1 *Photo, by courtesy of the Egypt Travel Bureau*

2 *Photo, Ricke*

3 *Photo, Ricke*

1. COPTIC CHURCH OF ABU SARGA, CAIRO
2. COPTIC CONVENT OF ABU MAKAR
3. COPTIC CONVENT OF SURIANI
4. THE WHITE MONASTERY, SOHAG

4 *Photo, Ricke*

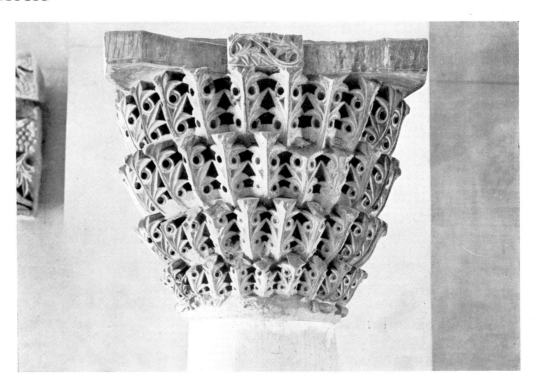

CAPITAL FROM BAOUIT   LOUVRE

CANOPY OF A NICHE FROM BAOUIT   LOUVRE

Photo, Exclusive News Agency

1. MONASTERY OF APA JEREMIAS, ALTAR AND WALL-PAINTING IN A CELL
   From Quibell, "Excavations at Saqqara."

2. CARVED WOOD PANEL FROM THE CHURCH OF ABU SARGA, CAIRO

3. PAINTING ON WOOD CHRIST AND A SAINT FROM BAOUIT, LOUVRE

PART OF A WALL-PAINTING OF A LION HUNT   BAOUIT

A CENTRAL CARVING OF A TYMPANUM
MOUNTED FIGURE OF A SAINT PIERCING A SERPENT
FROM BAOUIT   LOUVRE

1. WALL-DRAWING OF THE THREE HOLY CHILDREN   BRITISH MUSEUM

2. PAGE OF A SYNAXARY DATED A.D. 895   3. PAGE FROM A SYNAXARY DATED A.D. 914

FROM THE PIERPONT MORGAN LIBRARY (MSS. 577 & 597)   NEW YORK

1. PAGE FROM A BILINGUAL MS. OF
THE LITURGY, WRITTEN A.D. 1839

2. COPTIC BINDING FROM THE PIERPONT
MORGAN LIBRARY, NEW YORK

3. JOB AND HIS THREE DAUGHTERS   NAPLES

1. MEDALLION OF LINEN EMBROIDERED WITH
COLOURED SILKS. THE ANNUNCIATION AND
THE VISITATION   VIth-VIIth CENTURIES
Diameter 7½ ins.   VICTORIA & ALBERT MUSEUM

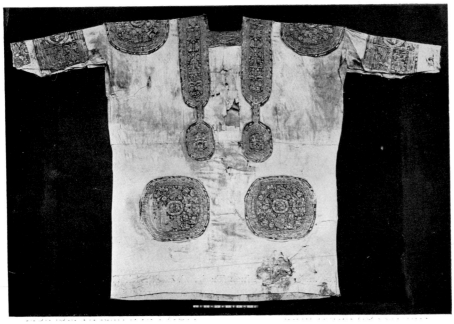

2. LINEN TUNIC WITH APPLIED TAPESTRY-WOVEN ORNAMENTS IN COLOURED
WOOLS AND UNDYED LINEN THREADS. PROBABLY FROM AKHMIM
VIth-VIIIth CENTURIES   Height 4 ft. 2 ins.   VICTORIA & ALBERT MUSEUM

1. Sleeve-Panel from a Linen Tunic. VIth-VIIIth Centuries

2. Portion of a Shoulder Band from a Linen Tunic. VIth-VIIth Centuries
From Akhmim

3. Sleeve-Panel from a Linen Tunic. VIth-VIIIth Centuries

TAPESTRY-WOVEN PANELS IN COLOURED WOOLS AND UNDYED LINEN
THREADS ON LINEN WARP   VICTORIA & ALBERT MUSEUM

PORTION OF A BAND OF TAPESTRY-WOVEN ORNAMENT IN WOOL
FROM THE LOWER EDGE OF A LINEN TUNIC   VIth—VIIth CENTURIES

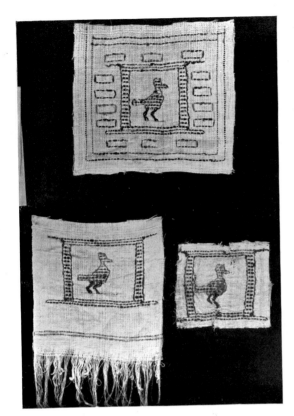

COPTIC TEXTILES FROM AKHMIM

BIRMINGHAM

1. MODEL OF A COPTIC CHURCH   FITZWILLIAM MUSEUM, CAMBRIDGE

2. BRONZE CENSER FROM THE
MONASTERY OF EPIPHANIUS

3 INLAID BRONZE BOX
COLLECTION OF M. RALPH HARARI

MUSLIM ARCHITECTURE

FROM A.D. 640

MOSQUE OF IBN ṬŪLŪN, BUILT A.D. 876-879. THE NORTH-EASTERN AISLE

MOSQUE OF IBN ṬŪLŪN, BUILT A.D. 876-879, THE OLDEST EXISTING MOSQUE IN EGYPT

The mosque proper, an arcaded courtyard, five arcades deep on the Mekka side, and two arcades deep on the other sides, is surrounded on three sides by a *ziyāda*, or open court, in which stands the spiral minaret.

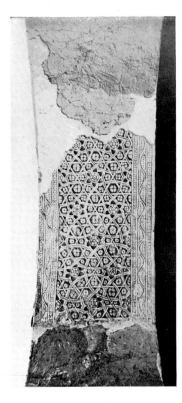

MOSQUE OF IBN ṬŪLŪN

1. One of the original stucco grilles in the sanctuary.
2-4. Stucco decoration of soffits of arches of south-western portico. A very early example of Muslim geometrical ornament.

One of the original stucco grilles in the back wall of the sanctuary.

Arcades of the sanctuary.

Detail of the repeat pattern which runs round all the arches of the sanctuary.

MOSQUE OF IBN ṬŪLŪN

266

MOSQUE OF AL-AZHAR, BUILT A.D. 970-972

The upper illustration shows the interior of the sanctuary, five aisles deep, cut through its centre by a transept, and the lower illustration shows this ornament in detail. It is most important, for it is the earliest Fāṭimid ornament known.

THE BĀB AN-NAṢR, BUILT A.D. 1087

One of the three Fāṭimid gates of Cairo, built by three Armenians from Edessa (Urfa) by order of the Fāṭimid Wazīr, Badr al-Gamālī, himself an Armenian.

THE NORTH WALL OF CAIRO

Part of the fortifications of Cairo carried out by the Fāṭimid Wazīr, Badr al-Gamālī,
between A.D. 1087 and 1092.   On the left is the Bāb an-Naṣr.

THE BĀB AL-FUTŪḤ (see next plate)

Showing the dome on spherical triangle pendentives which covers the passage way.

269

THE BĀB AL-FUTŪḤ

One of the three Fāṭimid gates of Cairo, built between A.D. 1087 and 1092, by three Armenian architects from Edessa (Urfa) by order of the Fāṭimid Wazīr, Badr al-Gamālī, himself an Armenian

THE BĀB ZUWEYLA, BUILT A.D. 1092

One of the three Fāṭimid gates of Cairo, built by three Armenian architects from Edessa, by order of the Fāṭimid Wazīr, Badr al-Gamālī, himself an Armenian.

271

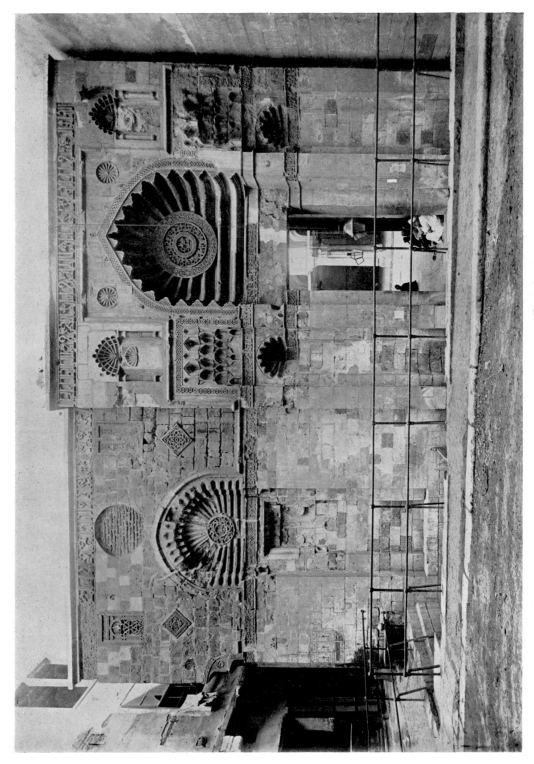

THE MOSQUE OF AL-AQMAR, BUILT A.D. 1125

Very important as the first mosque in Egypt with a monumental façade. This façade is symmetrical, the entrance being in the centre, and the right wing hidden behind a house.

MAIN MIHRĀB IN THE MAUSOLEUM OF SAYEDA RUQAYYA, BUILT A.D. 1133

A masterpiece of Fāṭimid stucco work, measuring 18 feet in height and 9 feet 8 inches in width.

THE CITADEL OF CAIRO, BEGUN BY SALADIN IN 1176 AND COMPLETED IN 1184

The Citadel consisted of two enclosures, a military enclosure strongly fortified, and a Palace enclosure without flanking defences. The former, which measures about 550 by 330 metres, is shown here, the view having been taken from the Muqaṭṭam, or rock cliff, which shuts in the Nile Valley on the East. The square towers are reinforcements due to Saladin's brother and successor al-'Ādil in 1207. The great round tower on the left is much later.

THE CITADEL OF CAIRO (see last plate)

The noble southern façade of the northern, or military enclosure, showing the reinforcements of al-ʿĀdil. The scale may be realised if one bears in mind that the great square tower in the centre measures over 98 feet square, or two feet more than the great keep of Norwich Castle.

MAUSOLEUM OF THE IMĀM ASH-SHĀF'EI, BUILT IN A.D. 1211

The dome is a single shell of wood with the ribs outside, the whole being covered with lead. At the summit is a bronze finial in the form of a boat.

MAUSOLEUM OF THE IMĀM ASH-SHĀF'EI, BUILT A.D. 1211 (see last plate)

Detail (telephoto) showing the beautiful stucco ornament on the exterior of the zone of transition between the square mausoleum and the circular base of the dome.

MAUSOLEUM OF THE 'ABBĀSID KHALIFS, BUILT ABOUT A.D. 1242

The miḥrāb shown here is one of the finest specimens of Ayyubid stucco ornament.

MOSQUE OF SULTAN BAYBARS, BUILT TO THE NORTH OF CAIRO, A.D. 1266-1269

A square, with a monumental entrance in three of its faces, the finest being the north-western one shown here.

THE MADRASA AND MAUSOLEUM OF SULTAN QALĀŪN, BUILT ON THE WEST
SIDE OF THE MAIN STREET OF MEDIEVAL CAIRO, IN A.D. 1284-1285

Beyond to the right is the Madrasa of Sultan Barqūq (dome and minaret), built A.D. 1384-1386

THE MAUSOLEUM OF SULTAN QALĀŪN, A.D. 1284-1285 (see last plate)

The top storey of the minaret was built by Qalāūn's son in A.D. 1304, after the great earthquake of 1303. It is one of several examples of Andalusian influence, noticeable in Cairo at the end of the thirteenth century, as a result of the great exodus of Muslims from Spain, which took place during this century owing to the extensive conquest of the Catholic Kings.

MAUSOLEUM OF THE EMĪRS SALĀR AND SANGAR AL-GĀWLĪ, A.D. 1303

The three arches, filled with beautiful stone grilles, light the passage which gives access to the mausoleums. The whole forms a really charming architectural composition.

THE MAUSOLEUM OF THE EMĪR SUNQŪR SA'DĪ, A.D. 1315

The finest example existing of a dome and its zone of transition decorated internally
and externally with stucco ornament.

283

THE MOSQUE OF THE EMĪR ALTUNBUGHĀ AL-MĀRIDĀNĪ, BUILT A.D. 1339-1340

Showing the great domed bay in front of the mihrāb, the third example of its kind.   (First example :
Mosque of Baybars, 1266-1269 ; second example : Mosque of Sultan an-Nāṣir Muhammad in the
Citadel, 1335).

TWO FINE EXAMPLES OF POLY-
CHROMY

1. Entrance to the Bath of the Emīr Beshtāk
   (d. 1341), and

2. Mausoleum of Princess Toghāī (d. 1348),
   drum of dome, one of the few examples
   of faience mosaic in Cairo.

MADRASA-MAUSOLEUM OF SULTAN HASAN, 1356-1362

View from the south-east, showing the great salient formed by the mausoleum. The original dome was a bulbous one, of wood. The minaret on the left is the tallest in Cairo (285 feet).

THE MIGHTY PORTAL OF THE MADRASA- MAUSOLEUM OF SULTAN HASAN
(see last plate)

287

MADRASA-MAUSOLEUM OF SULTAN HASAN (see pp. 286-287)

A view of the court showing the great līwāns, the main minaret and the domed fountain. The vault on the left is nearly as large as the great vault of Ctesiphon (height 83 feet 4 inches, against 89 feet 5 inches for Ctesiphon).

MONASTERY AND MAUSOLEUM OF SULTANS BARQŪQ AND FARAG, BUILT A.D. 1400-1410

This is a good example of a complex Mamlūk building, for it comprises two mausoleums, a mosque, a monastery for Sufis, a sebil (fountain) and a kuttāb (primary school). Almost the only structure of its kind with two minarets.

MONASTERY AND
MAUSOLEUM OF
SULTANS BARQŪQ
AND FARAG, BUILT
A.D. 1400-1410
(see last plate)

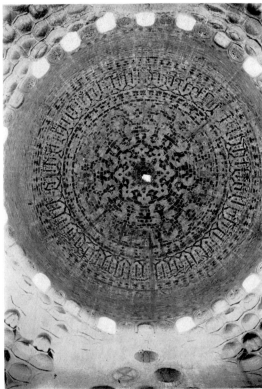

1. The east corner of the courtyard, showing the mausoleum of Sultan Barqūq and part of the mosque.
2. A vertical view of the dome of Sultan Farag's mausoleum. Note the stalactite pendentives and the polychrome decoration of the dome.

MONASTERY AND MAUSOLEUM OF SULTANS BARQŪQ AND FARAG

View of the sanctuary showing the magnificent stone pulpit (minbar) made by order of Sultan Qāyt-Bāy,
May-June 1483.

MOSQUE OF GŌHAR AL-LĀLĀ, A FREED SLAVE OF SULTAN BARSBĀY, BUILT
A.D. 1430

An example of a mosque built, not after the old arcaded courtyard type, but on the plan of a
madrasa of two līwāns. Note the splendid decoration of the back wall.

MADRASA-MAUSOLEUM OF SULTAN QĀYT-BĀY (FROM THE EAST), BUILT
A.D. 1470-1474

Another example of a complex Mamlūk building, comprising a mausoleum (under the dome), a
madrasa, or theological college, and, to the left of the entrance, a drinking fountain (sebīl) surmounted
by a primary school for boys (kuttāb).

MADRASA-MAUSOLEUM OF SULTAN QĀYT-BĀY, BUILT A.D. 1470-1474
(see last plate)

An unusual view taken from the north-east.

MOSQUE OF SĪNAN PASHA, AT BŪLĀQ, BUILT A.D. 1573   A fine example of the early Turkish period.

A square domed prayer chamber surrounded on three sides by a portico roofed with shallow domes.

THE MOSQUE OF MALIKA SĀFĪYA, BUILT A.D. 1610

The sanctuary, which is covered by a dome resting on six columns, is preceded by a cloistered courtyard with an entrance in each face approached by a flight of steps. The upper illustration shows the south-western entrance the lower the interior of the mosque.

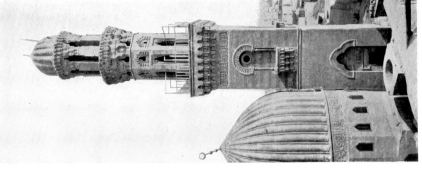

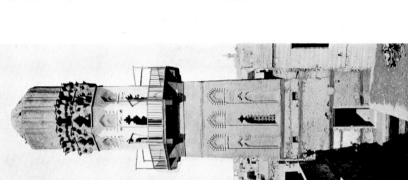

(1) MOSQUE OF AL-GUYŪSHĪ,
A.D. 1085

(2) MAUSOLEUM OF ABU'L-
GHADANFAR, A.D. 1155

(3) MADRASA OF SULTAN
SĀLIH, A.D. 1242

(4) MADRASA-MAUSOLEUM
of SALĀR AND SANGAR AL-
GĀWLĪ, A.D. 1303

The evolution of that somewhat rare type of Egyptian minaret with storeys which are successively square, octagonal and circular. This sequence shows that it has been produced by the gradual elongation and elaboration of the little domed pavilion at the summit of al-Guyūshī's minaret. The Pharos theory must therefore be given up.

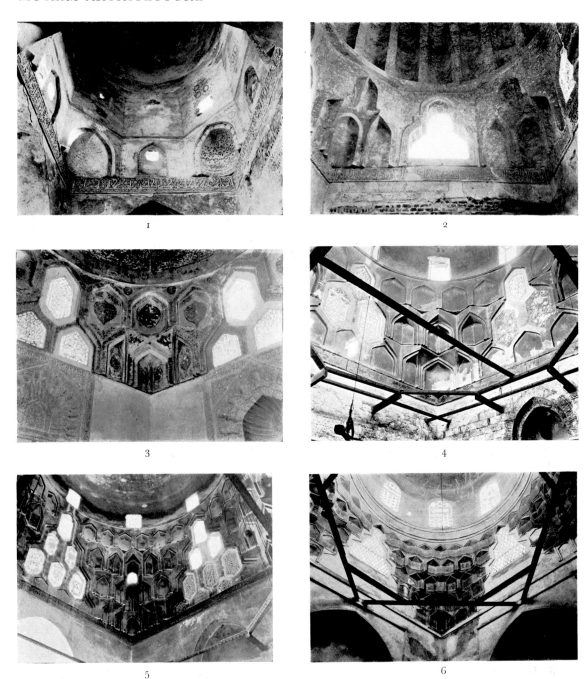

THE EVOLUTION OF THE EGYPTIAN STALACTITE PENDENTIVE

(1) Mosque of al-Guyūshī, A.D. 1085, showing the dome set on simple squinches. (2) Mausoleum of Muhammad al-Ga'farī, c. A.D. 1120 : the squinch has been, so to speak, shrunk into the corner and flanked by supplementary niches, the whole being surmounted by a fourth set forward slightly.

(3) The Mausoleum of the 'Abbāsid Khalifs, c. A.D. 1242 : the treatment already observed in the mausoleum of al-Ga'farī is repeated here, but the blank spaces of the upper tier are treated as niches. (4) Mausoleum of Sultan Sālih, A.D. 1250 : the dome in this case is considerably larger than the preceding, so a more gradual transition was required. The pendentive employed above is repeated here, but an extra tier of four niches has been placed above it.

(5) Mausoleum of Sultan Baybars al-Gashankīr, A.D. 1306-1309. The first example of four tiers of niches.
(6) The Mausoleum of the Emīr Ṣarghatmish, A.D. 1356, the first example of five tiers of niches.

298

THE HOUSE OF GAMĀL AD-DĪN AZ-ZAHABĪ, CHIEF OF THE GUILD OF GOLDSMITHS,
BUILT A.D. 1637

View of courtyard showing the *Maq'ad*, or veranda, facing north (direction of the prevailing wind).

THE HOUSE OF GAMĀL AD-DĪN AZ-ZAHABĪ, CHIEF OF THE GOLDSMITHS' GUILD,
BUILT A.D. 1637 (see last plate)

View of the *qaʻā*, or main reception room. The window at the end projects over the street in the
form of a mashrabīya balcony.

THE MUZAFFERKHANA PALACE, BUILT AT THE END OF THE EIGHTEENTH CENTURY

The illustration on the left shows one of the courtyards (the six ugly windows have replaced beautiful *mashrabiya*. The illustration on the right shows the T-shaped reception hall. The late Khedive Ismail was born in this palace in 1830.

THE MOSQUE OF MUHAMMAD ALY

(1) The Citadel, nobly crowned by the Mosque of Muhammad Aly, and (2) its slender minarets.

Photos, Exclusive News Agency

MUSLIM APPLIED ARTS

Photo by courtesy of Propyläen-Verlag, Berlin

BRONZE GRIFFIN
XIth CENTURY

CAMPO SANTO
PISA

DECORATED QURAN PAGE
MAMLUK PERIOD

COLLECTION OF
A. CHESTER BEATTY, ESQ.

MARBLE FLAG STONE
FOUND IN THE CONVENT
OF SULTAN BAIBARS II.
ON THE SITE OF THE
FATIMID VIZIER'S
PALACE
XIth CENTURY
ARAB MUSEUM CAIRO

1. WOOD PANEL DECORATED WITH SCROLLS
AND A VOTIVE KUFIC INSCRIPTION
IXth CENTURY

ARAB MUSEUM
CAIRO

2. WOOD PANEL DECORATED WITH SCROLLS
AND A PAIR OF PIGEONS
Xth CENTURY

ARAB MUSEUM
CAIRO

3. FRAGMENT OF A FRIEZE IN CARVED WOOD
FROM THE ROYAL PALACE OF THE FATIMIDS
Xth CENTURY

ARAB MUSEUM
CAIRO

ARAB MUSEUM, CAIRO

WOODEN PANELS FROM THE DOORS OF THE ROYAL PALACE OF THE FATIMIDS
Xth CENTURY

CARVED WOOD MIHRAB
FROM THE MAUSOLEUM
OF SAIYDA RUKAIYA
XIIth CENTURY
ARAB MUSEUM, CAIRO

1. IMPOST OF A DOOR OR WINDOW FROM THE MAUSOLEUM OF SAIYIDA NAFISA   ARAB MUSEUM, CAIRO
   XIIIth CENTURY

2. IVORY PANEL CARVED WITH AN INSCRIPTION IN THE NAME OF SULTAN QAIT BAY
   XVth CENTURY   ARAB MUSEUM, CAIRO

MIMBAR OF THE MOSQUE OF ABD EL GHARI FAKHRI
XVth CENTURY

CAIRO

MASHRABIYA WINDOW IN THE COURT-YARD
OF A HOUSE. (Now destroyed)
XVIIIth CENTURY

ENGRAVED BRONZE LION
Xth-XIth CENTURIES

VICTORIA AND ALBER
MUSEUM

BRONZE EWER IN THE SHAPE OF A PEACOCK
Xth-XIth CENTURIES   LOUVRE

1. BRONZE FALCON
HARARI COLLECTION

2. BRASS BOX
INLAID WITH
GOLD & SILVER
XIIIth CENTURY
VICTORIA AND
ALBERT MUSEUM

314

WOODEN DOORS WITH OPEN-WORK BRONZE
PLATING, BEARING THE NAME OF SULTAN
SUNQUR. FROM THE MOSQUE AT KHANQA
XIIIth CENTURY

ARAB
MUSEUM
CAIRO

BRASS TRAY INLAID WITH SILVER WITH
THE NAME OF SULTAN SHAABAN
XIVth CENTURY

BRITISH MUSEUM

BRONZE INCENSE-BURNER INLAID WITH SILVER
BEARING THE NAME OF MUHAMMAD IBN QALAUN
XIVth CENTURY

VICTORIA
AND ALBERT
MUSEUM

BRASS CISTERN INLAID WITH GOLD AND SILVER
BEARING THE NAME OF MUHAMMAD IBN QALAUN
XIVth CENTURY

BRITISH MUSEUM

GILT AND ENAMELLED GLASS MOSQUE LAMP
XIVth CENTURY

BRITISH MUSEUM

ENGRAVED BRASS CISTERN BEARING
THE NAME OF QAIT BAY
XVth CENTURY

HARARI COLLECTION

BRONZE VASE IN THE SHAPE OF
A MOSQUE LAMP
XIVth CENTURY   HARARI COLLECTION

BRONZE CANDLESTICK INLAID WITH SILVER
XIVth CENTURY

VICTORIA AND ALBERT MUSEUM

BRONZE CHANDELIER
INLAID WITH SILVER
BEARING THE NAME
OF QAIT BAY
XVth CENTURY
VICTORIA AND ALBERT
MUSEUM

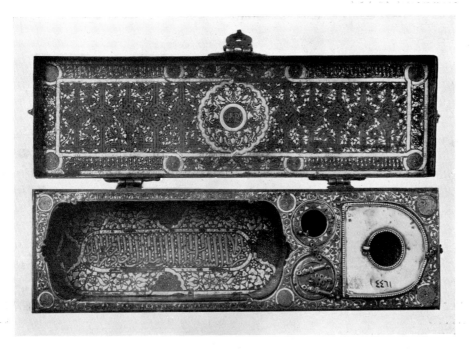

1. BRASS WRITING-CASE INLAID WITH GOLD AND SILVER   ARAB MUSEUM
   XIVth CENTURY   CAIRO

2. WOODEN QURAN-BOX, PLATED WITH BRONZE
   INLAID WITH GOLD AND SILVER FROM THE
   MAUSOLEUM OF SULTAN EL GHOURI   ARAB MUSEUM
   XIVth CENTURY   CAIRO

1. FRAGMENT OF POLYCHROME WOOLLEN FABRIC   ARAB MUSEUM
   Xth CENTURY   CAIRO

2. FRAGMENT OF LINEN FABRIC DECORATED   ARAB MUSEUM
   WITH BIRDS IN POLYCHROME   CAIRO
   XIIth CENTURY

1. FRAGMENT OF LINEN FABRIC, DECORATED
   WITH VOTIVE INSCRIPTIONS
   XIVth CENTURY

ARAB MUSEUM
CAIRO

2. FRAGMENT OF PALE GREEN SILK FABRIC
   WITH THE NAME OF MUHAMMAD IBN QALAUN
   XIVth CENTURY

VICTORIA AND
ALBERT MUSEUM

Photo, Cartier, Ltd.

FATIMID JEWELLERY
XIth-XIIth CENTURIES

HARARI COLLECTION

BRONZE STAG
Xth-XIth CENTURIES

NATIONAL MUSEUM
MUNICH

PLASTER FRAME FOR A COLOURED GLASS WINDOW
EARLY XIXth CENTURY

MUSLIM CERAMICS

ROCK CRYSTAL EWER
Xth-XIth CENTURIES

VICTORIA & ALBERT MUSEUM

1. LUSTRED FAIENCE DISH DECORATED
WITH A RIGGED GALLEY WITH OARS
IXth CENTURY

ARAB MUSEUM
CAIRO

2. FRAGMENT OF LUSTRED FAIENCE
DECORATED WITH A HEAD OF CHRIST
Xth-XIth CENTURIES

ARAB MUSEUM
CAIRO

LUSTRED FAIENCE DISH DECORATED
WITH THE FIGURE OF A MAN
SWINGING A CENSER

COLLECTION OF M. DIKRAN KELEKIAN
DEPOSITED ON LOAN AT THE
VICTORIA & ALBERT MUSEUM

1. FRAGMENT OF LUSTRED FAIENCE
   DECORATED WITH A SCENE FROM
   THE LIFE OF ABU TALIB, THE
   UNCLE OF THE PROPHET
   Xth-XIth CENTURIES
   ARAB MUSEUM, CAIRO

2. FAIENCE BOWL WITH INCISED
   DECORATION
   XIVth CENTURY
   COLLECTION OF M. DIKRAN
   KELEKIAN
   DEPOSITED ON LOAN AT THE
   VICTORIA & ALBERT MUSEUM

LUSTRED FAIENCE VASE DECORATED
WITH THREE BIRDS
Xth-XIth CENTURIES

COLLECTION OF M. DIKRAN KELEKIAN
DEPOSITED ON LOAN AT THE
VICTORIA & ALBERT MUSEUM

LUSTRED FAIENCE VASE
DECORATED WITH FISHES
Xth-XIth CENTURIES

COLLECTION OF M. DIKRAN KELEKIAN
DEPOSITED ON LOAN AT THE
VICTORIA & ALBERT MUSEUM

FRAGMENTS OF BLUE FAIENCE
WITH UNDERGLAZE DECORATION
XIVth CENTURY

ARAB MUSEUM
CAIRO

1. PANEL OF POLYCHROME MARBLE MOSAIC　　　　　　　ARAB MUSEUM, CAIRO

2. FAIENCE DISC BEARING THE
NAME OF SULTAN QAIT BAY　　　　　　　ARAB MUSEUM
XVth CENTURY　　　　　　　　　　　　　　CAIRO

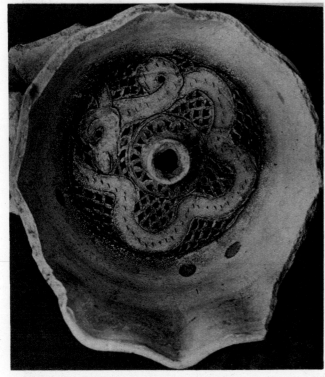

GARGOULETTE FILTERS.

ARAB MUSEUM, CAIRO

1. FRAGMENT OF A CUT GLASS BOWL
   IXth-Xth CENTURIES   ARAB MUSEUM, CAIRO

2. FRAGMENT OF ENAMELLED GLASS   ARAB MUSEUM
   SHEWING CHINESE INFLUENCE   CAIRO

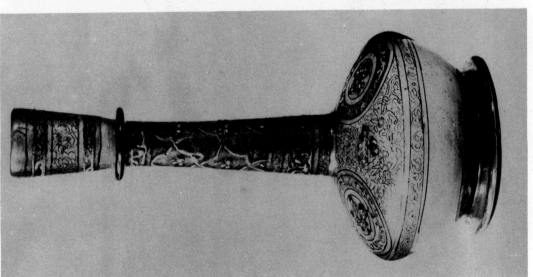

1.	2.	3.

ENAMELLED GLASS FLAGONS
XIIIth-XIVth CENTURIES

1. & 2. ARAB MUSEUM, CAIRO
3. VICTORIA & ALBERT MUSEUM

ENAMELLED GLASS MOSQUE LAMP
XIVth CENTURY

VICTORIA & ALBERT MUSEUM

ENAMELLED GLASS MOSQUE LAMP
XIVth CENTURY

VICTORIA & ALBERT MUSEUM

2. LARGE ENAMELLED GLASS FLAGON
XIVth CENTURY

VICTORIA & ALBERT MUSEUM

1. ENAMELLED GLASS VASE
XIVth CENTURY

COLLECTION OF
H.H. PRINCE YOUSSEF KAMAL

CONCLUSION

"Egypt . . . was beyond all dispute, for all people and to all time, the parent of Geometry, Astronomy, Architecture and Chivalry. She was, in its material and technic elements, the mistress of Literature, showing authors who before could only scratch on wax and wood, how to weave paper and engrave porphyry."

JOHN RUSKIN, *The Bible of Amiens*

WE have surveyed in a few chapters six thousand years of history and four great civilisations—the Pharaonic, the Alexandrine, the Christian (or Coptic-Byzantine) and the Muslim. Each of these periods is so distinct from the others as apparently to belong to a different country and to express the genius of a different nation. Egypt has witnessed the coming and going of conquering races, and they have left such a deep imprint on its soil that the Valley of the Nile is a true record of the succeeding epochs in the history of mankind ; yet an original and native element has survived throughout these superimposed cultures, manifesting itself more especially in the craft of weavers and potters.

"One may endeavour," writes A. J. Butler,[1] " to show that the continuity of ceramic tradition in the valley of the Nile was unbroken, up to the Arab conquest, and that while method and process remained unaltered, the old spirit and skill sometimes veering to new forms and developments, sometimes impaired by the lapse of centuries, yet lived and revived in the Muhammadan period."

The same remark applies to the textiles. "An exact determination of the date of the various groups of Islamic material is extremely difficult. . . . These latter are generally based on the technique and themes of an old tradition and repeat, unchanged, the same forms for many hundred years. That is especially true of a great mass of embroideries where it is very difficult to differentiate exactly between Coptic, Fatimid and Mamluk products."[2]

Moreover, in default of a continuous tradition, that which one finds in Egypt is the constant relation of architecture to the landscape, climate and atmosphere, the definite influence of the local technique and of the materials employed.

It is that which gives their original character to certain monuments of the Muhammadan period, such as the mosque of Sultan Hasan, though Islamic art has always had a universal character. Delicate, intricate, of exquisite

[1] Islamic pottery.
[2] Volbach and Kuehnel. Late antique, Coptic and Islamic textiles.

colouring in Persia, rich in line, vivid in hue, ornate and sumptuous in Spain, Muslim architecture is, in Egypt, sombre, stately and restrained in its use of decoration.

Egypt is in duration as it is in space a river flowing from the remoteness of time, from sources unknown, and never wholly losing itself in the sands. In spite of the continual intrusion of foreign elements, the fellah has preserved a sameness and fixity of type. Even the animals are unchanged—the oxen display to-day the characteristics depicted in Pharaonic frescoes.[3]

Egypt was the converging point of the Ancient world, the meeting place of Eastern and Western cultures. Yet she herself exerted a steady influence over her neighbours. The armies of Thutmosis and of Ramses spread far and wide the tendencies of Pharaonic art and traces of it are still found from Moghreb to Persia and from Scythia to Central Africa.[4] The lyrical inspiration of the Hebrews, and the artistic genius of the Greeks sprung thence. " Egypt," wrote Ruskin, " was beyond all dispute, for all people and to all time, the parent of Geometry, Astronomy, Architecture and Chivalry. She was, in its material and technic elements, the mistress of Literature, showing authors who before could only scratch on wax and wood, how to weave paper and engrave porphyry. She was the first exponent of the Law of Judgment after Death for Sin. She was the Tutress of Moses and the Hostess of Christ."

A monument of the Third Dynasty has been discovered at Sakkara with fluted columns which foreshadow the shafts of the Doric order. I can find no better way of describing it than quoting the words of Princess Bibesco. " I have found," she says, " the birth-place of Greek art . . . Imothep, architect of King Zozer, was the first to use freestone in Egypt. The inscription tells that he was placed among the gods for having built these temples. It is no wonder. They are divine, more beautiful than that of the Wingless Victory on the Acropolis, which they resemble, with something more finished, more compact in their perfection. They date about thirty centuries before Phidias. Looking at them, I feel more keenly the aristocratic order which rules our inheritance. Egypt holds precedence. Those who upheld the free art of the Greeks against the slavish art of the Egyptians must hang their heads in shame since the discovery of the Sakkara columns."[5]

Indeed, the art of Ancient Egypt was scarcely appreciated by the archæologists and historians of the nineteenth century. Vogüé believed it to be essentially " realistic." Maspéro held that all forms in Egypt—architecture, sculpture and painting—tended not towards " the search for the beautiful " but towards " the realisation of the useful," and Renan looked upon Egypt as " a China born old and almost decrepit, at once childish and senile ; a

---

[3] See Schweinfurth.
[4] See Elliot-Smith and Perry.
[5] Jour d'Egypte.

land of clear and rapid consciousness, but a consciousness which is limited and static."

Yet all these notions of monotony, conventionality, pompousness, heavyness, ornateness, realism, with which Egyptian art was indiscriminately labelled, are only true of the worst works of the later periods, when a degenerate and bastard form appeared. They do not apply to the monuments of the early dynasties, with their sober and powerful lines, nor to the classical sculpture of the twelfth century, nor to that exquisite flowering of the Amarna period when a search for plastic refinement and subtlety replaced the austerity of the early masters. " Faces treated before in an architectonic way, begin to reflect inner emotion ; the diffuse light now centres on eyelids and lips. The skin seems living and delicately transparent under the eyes. The dramatic pathos of movement is a new element, which serves to express the personality of the king (Akhnaton), whose hidden traits captivated the artist."[6]

A scribe of this epoch formulated his theory of æsthetics in terms which neither Cézanne nor El-Greco would have rejected : " Art lies in balance of straight lines and curves, cubes and cones." Never have " the values of mass, space and line " (as Scott says) " been more coherently displayed." Sculpture and painting in Egypt were subordinated to architecture as they are in the Gothic cathedrals. Beyond Græco-Roman paganism, the Gothic soul is heir to the spirit of Ancient Egypt. Both the medieval craftsmen and the ancient cutters of granite found their means of expression in the symbolic power of stone. Rodin and Bourdelle have discovered Egyptian affinities in the work of the sculptors of Chartres.

One cannot say of Egypt that it was " pagan " in the narrow sense of the word. More than Hellenic art, Egyptian art carries us away from earthly realities. This religious character seems to have always been one of the traits of the Egyptians. Claude Field wrote in his " Mystics and saints of Islam " : " Egypt has always been a soil favourable to the development of mystic tendencies. Christian ascetisism took early root there, and during the first centuries of our era thousands of Anchorities have inhabited the desert of the Thebaid, and carried on there religious practices of extreme austerity. We do not know what secret connection may exist between the climate of Egypt and its inhabitants, but, if the Arab chroniclers deserve any credit, Arab mysticism originated in this country."

Before the Byzantines the Egyptians discovered that the purpose of art lay not in the classical technique of reproduction, but in a " will to philosophic expression." It may be that the origins of Western painting should be sought beyond the Italian Renaissance and the tradition of Byzantine icons, in the frescoes of Baouit (which belong to the sixth and seventh centuries A.D.), the Fayoum portrait paintings on wood (which go back to the second century A.D.)

[6] J. Fechheimer.

and the conventionalised images of the dead on Pharaonic sarcophagi. As Robert Byron writes,[7] El-Greco preserved " a tradition whose style . . . may still be seen on icons in the (Greek) churches of Egypt." And Stephen Gaselee, in his chapter on the art of the Coptic period, states that "if the Coptic frescoes at the monastery of St. Jeremias at Sakkara be placed alongside of the (rather later) frescoes of Constantinople, they have little to fear ; the figure of Christ, at once Saviour and Judge, usually found in the narthex, attains a kind of sublimity, combining majesty and tenderness in a manner hardly equalled elsewhere."

Emile Mâle has pointed out that the Coptic frescoes of Baouit inspired the twelfth century sculptures of the Monastery of Moissac ; while the slender columns of Baouit, the capitals with their acanthus leaves, their Greek key pattern ornaments (so light that they seem more like linear drawing than like bas-relief) foreshadow the Saxon and Romanesque decorative patterns. In his remarkable " Aesthetics of proportions in Art and Nature," Matila Ghyka quotes medieval traditions which ascribe an Egyptian origin to certain architectural rules ; and it is possible that the traditions of Masonry, with their esoteric science of numbers, derive from Pharaonic times. Did not Viollet-le-Duc claim that " the key to the vertical structure in many Gothic cathedrals is an isosceles triangle borrowed from the proportions of the Great Pyramid ? " This triangle may have been transmitted to the architects of the West by Crusaders who had come in contact with Arab monuments, inspired in their turn by the school which had flourished in Alexandria just before the rise of Islam.

When the Arabs conquered Alexandria, it contained (Amrou tells us) " 4,000 palaces, 4,000 baths and 400 theatres " and " the lighthouse—the Pharos—was still perfect and functioned for a few years more." " Nor were the Arabs," adds E. M. Forster, " content with praising the lighthouse : they even looked at it. ' El Manarah ' as they called it, gave the name to, and became the model for, the minaret, and one can still find minarets in Egypt that exactly reproduce the design of Sostratus—the bottom storey square, second octagonal, third round."

In his " Introduction to Persian Art " Dr. Pope shows us " the industrious Copts " working for the Arab conquerors of Persia, and points out how the floral motifs and the geometrical resources of the abstract decoration were enriched by the elaboration of Græco-Roman mosaic designs " at the hands of workmanlike and industrious Copts."

As to the influence of Saracenic art on the West, either through Spain or carried by the Crusaders, it has often been noted. It was brought, moreover, by pilgrims and travellers, and a description of the palace of a Fatimid Sultan of Cairo, in the twelfth century, by William of Tyre shows us the amazement of a man of the West faced with such magnificence.

[7] Robert Byron. " The Birth of Western Painting."

" The ambassadors passed through courts and passages, through colonnades and marble porticoes with gilded ceilings and many coloured floors ; so that the whole was marked there with royal splendour. The material and workmanship were so precious that the two envoys could hardly cease to contemplate the sight, the perfection of which surpassed anything that they had seen before. There were fishpools of marble filled with purest water, birds of all kinds, unknown to us, with strange voices, shapes and hues and of marvellous appearance. Thence they were led by Eunuchs into other halls, exceeding the first in beauty. They saw a multitude of quadrupeds such as the countries of the East and South alone produce, which the West never sees and of which it hears only rarely."

According to Makrisi, the Caliph Mostanser possessed in the eleventh century 18,000 crystal vases, of which some were valued at more than a thousand dinars ; 400 cages and 600 vessels of gold, 22,000 amber jewels, tables of sardonix, golden cocks, peacocks, gazelles studded with pearls and rubies, a garden with soil of vermilion, paths of amber, silver trees and fruit of precious stones.

Heir to all this, Egypt went through a long period of decline since the Ottoman conquest, in 1517, and revived only after its political regeneration under the House of Muhammad-Aly. Archæological researches, excavation and scientific survey of Pharaonic monuments, collection of ancient Egyptian masterpieces in the Museum of Antiquities, the creation of a National Library and gathering together of precious illuminated manuscripts hitherto scattered and lost sight of, the foundation of an Arab Museum to house the treasures of the Fatimids, Ayoubids and Mamluks, the restoration of Mosques and of other architectural wonders of the Muslim period, were all begun in the reign of the Khedive Ismail, and since his time this work has been carried on by the élite of the country. A Græco-Roman museum has been opened in Alexandria, and a Coptic Museum in Cairo founded on the actual sight of the " Moalaka " church. How much has been done by Egypt's present sovereign, King Fuad I, is an open secret. It has been his constant effort to inspire in the hearts of his subjects a still greater pride in the traditions of their country, for, as he said in 1911, when he inaugurated the Egyptian University : " It is only when a people earnestly cultivates its feelings of veneration for its ancestors and the deeds of its own heroes that it learns and appreciates to the full the secret of its own destiny."

INDEX TO ILLUSTRATIONS